CIVIL WAR LEXINGTON, KENTUCKY

CIVIL WAR LEXINGTON, KENTUCKY

Bluegrass Breeding Ground of Power

JOSHUA H. LEET &
KAREN M. LEET

THE
History
PRESS

Published by The History Press
Charleston, SC 29403
www.historypress.net

Front cover: *Main & Limestone; Lexington, KY, 1860*, Wilson Family Photographic Collection, PA62W8, Special Collections, University of Kentucky.
Back cover: Paintings of Jefferson Davis and Henry Clay, by William P. Welsh, courtesy of Transylvania University.

First published 2011
ISBN 978-1-5402-3047-8

Library of Congress Cataloging-in-Publication Data
Leet, Joshua H.
Civil War Lexington, Kentucky : Bluegrass breeding ground of power / Joshua H. Leet and Karen M. Leet.
p. cm.
Includes bibliographical references and index.
ISBN 978-1-5402-3047-8
1. Lexington (Ky.)--History--19th century. 2. Kentucky--History--Civil War, 1861-1865.
3. United States--History--Civil War, 1861-1865. 4. Lexington (Ky.)--Biography. 5.
Kentucky--History--Civil War, 1861-1865--Biography. 6. United States--History--Civil War,
1861-1865--Biography. I. Leet, Karen M. II. Title.
F459.L6L44 2011
976.9'041--dc23
2011036889

Contents

CONTENTS

Acknowledgements

Our grateful appreciation to all the knowledgeable individuals who helped make this book possible, to all the experts and specialists who shared their wisdom with us and to all the historic site staff members who opened doors for us literally and figuratively. Thanks to the Lexington Public Library Kentucky Room; the University of Kentucky Special Collections; the Transylvania University Special Collections; the Lexington History Museum; the Hunt Morgan House; Ashland, the Henry Clay Estate; Waveland; the Mary Todd Lincoln House; the Lexington Cemetery; and the Bluegrass Trust for Historic Preservation.

We appreciate everyone's kindness and generosity, and we urge our readers to visit these valuable Bluegrass historical resources to learn more about Lexington and the men and women who had a Lexington connection. We also encourage each reader to dig deeper into the lives of the men and women introduced in our book—try some of the wonderful, extensive biographies that reveal further details about their lives, times and accomplishments.

Introduction

Athens of the West

L exington, Kentucky, produced no great battles during the Civil War, and consequently, its part in the great conflict is often overlooked. Instead, the city afforded to each side some of its greatest leaders, both on the field of battle and in the capitals of each nation. Lexington, Kentucky, Bluegrass breeding ground of power, produced the Honorable Henry Clay, and though he died before the Civil War began, his compromise efforts postponed the war by at least a decade. Lexington touched the lives of both Jefferson Davis, president of the Confederate States of America, and Abraham Lincoln, United States president, whose wife, Mary Todd, spent her early years there. Lexington molded the careers and characters of men like John C. Breckinridge, who served as senator, United States vice president, general and Confederate secretary of war for the final months of the conflict. These individuals and others like them helped shape the face of the war and the history of the United States. And each of these men and women was in some way influenced by or left their mark on the city of Lexington. Sons of Lexington, like John Hunt Morgan, Thunderbolt of the Confederacy, kept the homeplace in their hearts and would someday return to rest there at their journey's end.

In the early 1800s, Lexington, heart of the Bluegrass region, often called the Athens of the West, thrived and grew. Lush farmlands and rolling, grassy hillsides attracted families who would become part of Kentucky history for generations to come. With a major hemp industry and a wide range of

Lexington in 1850. *Courtesy of J. Winston Coleman Jr. Photographic Collection, Transylvania University.*

Transy in 1860. *Courtesy of Transylvania University Archives.*

businesses, Lexington became a bustling center for commerce. Transylvania, the oldest educational institution west of the Allegheny Mountains, drew students from the finest families across the West and South. With both law and medical departments, Transylvania produced statesmen, diplomats, governors, doctors and judges for the entire nation.

Lexington farms provided blooded horses that would later help fill the huge demand for mounts when cavalries of both North and South searched for the finest horseflesh available. Before the war, militia groups in Lexington drilled and paraded, showing their skills and elegant uniforms for the delight of townspeople. Those militia groups would form the basis for volunteers heading out to fight on both sides.

Lexington became a forum for political thought and excitement as Henry Clay repeatedly attempted to become United States president. A young Mary Todd would listen eagerly to lengthy political debates and discussions in her own home, showing an early fascination with the subject that would become a common ground between herself and a youthful Abraham Lincoln with political aspirations of his own.

Though Kentucky never seceded from the Union when war swept through the nation, the state and the city of Lexington had deep Southern roots, including maintaining what was called the "peculiar institution" of slavery. With Kentucky supposedly displaying a "mild" form of slavery, the institution held firm, with most affluent households depending on slave labor, including the homes of Henry Clay and Mary Todd. Downtown Lexington held court days where cattle, horses and slaves might be sold at auction equally casually. A slave whipping post was a standard feature, and citizens took the institution of slavery for granted as something they often considered evil but necessary.

By the time war spread across the nation, Lexington had suffered a decline. Members of prominent families sought better fortunes in the West. Attendance at Transylvania had fallen off to the point that the educational facility almost ceased existence entirely. Cholera epidemics in 1833 and 1849 carried off many hundreds of citizens and set back business and farm growth in the region.

When war broke out, Kentucky declared its neutrality, resolutely refusing to choose sides, but the state and the city of Lexington soon found that neutrality would not work. Though a group with Southern sympathies briefly established a Confederate capital and government, adding a star to the Confederate flag, Kentucky as a whole and Lexington in particular remained in the Union. Federal troops occupied the city of Lexington for most of the war, with occasional Confederate raids and a brief Confederate occupation for several weeks in 1862. As was the case throughout the country, families were split as allegiances were declared. For the most part, Lexington survived the war relatively unscathed, suffering only a few skirmishes and bouts of arson and looting. However, not every individual with ties to Lexington fared as well.

Chapter 1

The Great Compromiser

Henry Clay

S urely this time he would reach the goal he had sought so vigorously throughout his long and distinguished career. Surely this time the nation would turn its heart to him and choose him to lead the Union, to be the ultimate leader, to be president of the United States. Surely this time the race would be won. His friends and supporters worked tirelessly. He inspired that sort of dedication and energy from those who stood by him. The contest was tight, the results uncertain. As George Ranck said in the *History of Fayette County*, "This contest was one of the fiercest and most stubborn that had yet been waged in America." Yet when the thing ended, Henry Clay had lost yet again. It was his final chance, though he did not know it at the time. The year was 1844, and James K. Polk would step into the office Clay had hungered for so insistently.

Though born, raised and educated in Virginia, Henry Clay made his way to Lexington, Kentucky, to establish himself in his chosen profession, the law, though his interest in politics soon surfaced. Ranck pointed out that "Lexington was then the metropolis of the West," and in Lexington, Clay maintained his home base for the remainder of his career. He married Lucretia Hart, and together they had eleven children, only four of whom survived him. His magnificent home, Ashland, lay just outside the city and became a refuge for him whenever he returned from lengthy stays in Washington while he pursued his political career. Like Antaeus of Greek mythology who drew strength from the earth beneath his feet, Henry Clay seemed to draw his strength from his Bluegrass home.

Though he first pursued the law, local audiences soon came to appreciate his oratory skills. Henry Clay would become nationally known and admired for his natural talent at speech and debate. He spoke with drama and wit, able to poke an enemy's weakest points and confound those whose thought processes worked more slowly than his own. His political career began in his adopted home state as he entered the Kentucky legislature. During his lengthy career, he served as United States senator, Speaker of the House of Representatives and secretary of state under President John Quincy Adams. The last role would cost him dearly, according to Ranck, who noted, "It was charged that he had bought his seat in the cabinet, and the cry of 'bargain and corruption' was repeated over and over again to the end of his life, and defeated him in every subsequent race for the presidency."

The charges, which haunted Clay for the rest of his political life, stemmed from his first nomination for the presidency. The contest went to the House of Representatives, where Clay chose to throw his faltering candidacy over in

Henry Clay, statesman. *Courtesy of Library of Congress.*

favor of Adams, who then defeated opponents W.H. Crawford and Andrew Jackson. When Adams became president, he offered the cabinet post to Clay, who accepted. Being secretary of state traditionally opened the way to step into the presidency, so Clay saw this as a steppingstone to the office he truly yearned to fill. However, his enemies declared he'd thrown his vote to Adams as a way of "buying" a cabinet position.

Though Clay would again be chosen as his party's candidate for president two more times and would hope for the nomination even as late as 1848, this scandal hung over his head every time he reached for the top office. Historians wonder—had Clay been elected president in one of his frequent efforts, could he have reshaped the course of the nation? His skill at working out compromises earned him nicknames such as the Great Compromiser and the Great Pacificator. Henry Clay responded to his country's need for a peacemaker every time he was needed, and who can resist wondering if he had been alive in 1860, might he have somehow managed to head off the terrible Civil War entirely?

Harry of the West, campaign badge.
Courtesy of Library of Congress.

In between struggles to achieve the top office or to push some vital piece of legislation through a conflicted Congress, Clay headed home. He enjoyed his time spent at Ashland. He enjoyed breeding fine horses and looking out over the expanse of farmland he cultivated. His wife, who would mark fifty-plus years of marriage with him, demonstrated her strength and ability by managing the estate whenever he was in Washington or out of the country brokering peace agreements.

Lexington was home. Clay felt at peace when he came home, settling into a life of acclaim among the people who loved him most, surrounded by family and friends. Always suffering from health troubles, he found Ashland a refuge from the demands of Washington. He supported local institutions, such as Transylvania, where he served as trustee and faculty member in the law department.

In addition to his involvement in Lexington affairs and his long and fruitful years of political service, Clay also became head of an interesting organization, the American Colonization Society. He served as president of this organization until his death, and he sincerely believed in the group's purpose—to open an opportunity for free slaves to form their own colony on the continent of Africa. Clay saw this as a strong and hopeful solution to the slavery question. The organization raised funds, though it struggled to collect adequate amounts for its goals. Not only would it send freed slaves to Africa, but also it would provide funds to give each individual a start on a new life.

Clay, who termed himself a gradual emancipationist, owned slaves nearly his entire life. He spoke out against slavery, designating the peculiar institution to be evil, yet he lived in a state where slaveholding among the elite was the norm, where slavery was often verbally condemned by the same men who held slaves, sold them when times got tight and even rented them out to earn some extra income. Clay felt the same paternalistic tendencies common in his home state and across the South. Many slave owners believed that to free slaves with no education or preparation for a life on their own would be foolhardy and destructive.

Some slave owners who decried slavery set up elaborate plans for the eventual emancipation of the men, women and children they owned. Some declared they would free their slaves in their wills, with special arrangements for education and financial provision. Not every will was honored by the family. Other slave owners willed their slaves to Henry Clay and the American Colonization Society and left Clay to deal with the legal ramifications in slave states where laws complicated such actions. In correspondence, Clay worked out ways and means for sending those slaves willed to him or to the society to new homes in Africa, in the colony established there, Liberia. For those slaves who refused to relocate because they would not leave behind family members who had not been set free, the society tried to find solutions.

Clay himself realized what a fine line he walked between slave owner and emancipationist. In a letter to Horace Greeley, famed abolitionist, Clay remarked of his attempt to win his party's presidential nomination in 1848: "I presume my residence in a Slave State lost me the nomination." Clay must have realized that his stance as a gradual emancipationist worked against him in slave states like his home base of Kentucky, while his ownership of slaves worked against him with Northern abolitionists who wanted an end to slavery now, if not sooner, and would go to whatever lengths it took to free every slave immediately. Henry Clay struggled with a balancing act to try to appeal to such opposing viewpoints, and as some of his opponents noted, he failed to please either side.

In a letter responding to Joshua R. Giddings on October 6, 1847, Clay wrote, "You kindly refer to the subject of the slaves I hold, and tell me what would be the good consequences of my emancipating them." He went on to express his ambivalence: "I regret as much as any one does the existence of slavery in our country, and wish to God there was not a single slave in the United States, or in the whole world. But here the unfortunate institution is, and a most delicate and difficult affair it is to deal with." He explained, "I have during my life emancipated some eight or ten, under circumstances which appeared to me to admit of their emancipation…Of the remainder (some fifty odd), what I ought to do with them, and how, and when, is a matter of grave and serious consideration often with me." With the paternalistic attitude of many slave holders, Clay insists, "They would perish if I sent them forth in the world."

And so the conflict stood, with some slaveholders saying they wanted their slaves to be freed but not taking any action on their behalf, while Northern abolitionists agitated for freedom, sometimes instigating violence where they felt it would serve the greater good. Meanwhile, the nation had begun to expand as new territories petitioned to join the Union. With the South solidly in the slave column and the North hoping that slavery would die off of its own weight, the nation was being forced to confront the issue. Would slavery stay as a strictly Southern institution? Or would new territories and newly admitted states allow the spread of slavery?

Murmurs of possible secession and even war echoed through the nation as debate raged over whether new states would be admitted as slave states, free states or independent entities that could decide their own fate. Ranck noted Clay's "Herculean labors to avert the convulsion which threatened the nation in 1821 on the application of Missouri for admission into the Union." And despite the repeated losses Clay faced in his efforts to attain the highest office in the land, he exerted his substantial influence among lawmakers to hold the country together.

In a speech in 1844, Clay declared his love of country: "It has been my invariable rule to do all for the Union. If any man wants the key of my heart, let him take the key of the Union, and that is the key to my heart." When, in 1850, the nation teetered on the brink of dissolution, Clay shrugged off yet another loss in his bid for a presidential candidacy in 1848 to step forward on behalf of his nation. Adding new territories once more threatened the balance between slave states and free states. Those in the South, feeling compelled to maintain their rights as slaveholders, fought for slavery in the newest territories. Those in the North fought to prevent slavery expansion throughout the additional segments of the nation.

Clay stepped into the wrestling match with a set of compromises in which each section must sacrifice something for the sake of gaining something in return. He linked proposals together in such a way that each side felt it would receive fair treatment. Ranck mentioned Clay's "mighty efforts during the perilous slavery excitement in Congress in 1850–52." Tirelessly, Clay spoke out on behalf of his compromise plan. Steadily, he whittled away at complaints and quarrels among members of Congress. He spoke for hours on the House floor and worked his most persuasive charm in every direction.

Even so, as his health faltered, his efforts seemed to fall short. The nation seemed about to topple into war and disunion. Clay retreated in discouragement, while Senator Stephen Douglas maneuvered and pried at Congress until each portion of Clay's extensive compromise passed, item by item. Some new areas would decide about slavery for themselves. Laws like the Fugitive Slave Law would remain in place. The balancing act called for compromise on everyone's part. Yet because of Henry Clay's monumental efforts, the Union held.

This would be his final battle on the political field. His health continued to deteriorate until he died in Washington, D.C., in 1852. He would not live to see the Compromise of 1850 challenged almost a decade later. He would not live to see the Union he loved torn to shreds as Southern states declared their independence from the nation. He would not live to see a war that set brother against brother in his beloved home state of Kentucky, throughout the nation and even in his own family.

Henry Clay broke his heart and his health holding together the Union and struggling for his dream of reaching the White House. Was it proud ambition, as his enemies accused, that drove him to pursue the presidency so persistently? He reportedly announced he would rather be right than be

Henry Clay reviews troops. *Courtesy of Henry Clay Manuscript Collection, Transylvania University.*

president. Supposedly, his enemies proclaimed that he was neither. Or might his determination, so often and painfully thwarted, to be commander and chief be the result of a deep desire to save the nation he loved? No one now can know his heart. It's enough to know his hopes shattered when time after time the nation that seemed to adore him denied him the ultimate goal he sought. After each failure, the Bluegrass called him home to heal, regain strength and restore his courage, only to be wooed back to Washington yet again to serve his fellow citizens.

As Robert V. Rimini wrote in *Henry Clay: Statesman for the Union*, "He might have made a truly great President."

Chapter 2

He Also Ran

John Breckinridge

When the delegates for the Democratic Party met to choose their candidate for president of the United States for the 1860 election, dissension tore at the party. Slavery and states' rights had for decades reared up as divisive issues among Americans. With every new territory added to the country, heated debates flourished. Should slavery expand into the territories? Should states have the right to choose for themselves whether to approve slavery? Perhaps it boiled down to who would be in charge—individual states or the United States government.

Abraham Lincoln had made a name for himself nationally through the series of debates between him and Senator Stephen Douglas. The nation had heard Lincoln speak out against slavery, so when the Republican Party chose Lincoln, the Democrats searched for a strong candidate to oppose him. Unable to settle sectional differences among their delegates, the Northern members chose Douglas as their candidate, while the Southern delegates selected John C. Breckinridge to run for president. Though he hadn't sought the nomination and was then serving as vice president under Buchanan, Breckinridge did his best.

First, he tried to reunite his party. He felt that if both he and Douglas stepped down, the party might find another candidate strong enough to defeat Lincoln and hold the nation together. Breckinridge did not want war. Yet another candidate who would split the vote had entered the race, as well. John Bell ran as a Constitutional Unionist. If Breckinridge could persuade both Douglas and Bell to drop out and then drop out himself, perhaps a new candidate could pull together the Lincoln opposition and be strong enough to beat the "Old Rail Splitter."

When his plan did not bring about a withdrawal of the other candidates, Breckinridge fought hard for the office of president. He put his substantial oratory skills to work and exercised his considerable diplomatic talents to head off the Lincoln candidacy. He failed—his first political failure in an illustrious career. Lincoln won the election with a substantial majority. Lincoln's 180 electoral votes solidly outdid the accumulated votes of the other three candidates. Bell earned 39 electoral votes, Douglas got 12 and Breckinridge won 72.

As vice president, Breckinridge had the dubious honor of counting the votes and announcing that Lincoln had won the presidency. Though some with sectional prejudices mistrusted Breckinridge, fearing he would manage

Senator John C. Breckinridge. *Courtesy of Library of Congress.*

to lose some of Lincoln's votes, the vice president did his job and did it fairly and well. He might not have liked what he had to do, but he did it.

Unable to accomplish much as vice president, he welcomed his state's choice to send him to the United States Senate, where he worked hard to keep the nation together, representing the South in the minds of his fellow senators. He argued for states' rights and he argued for slavery being a property issue and nothing more. He felt the Constitution of the United States protected property rights and that since slaves were property, bought and paid for, the Constitution protected the South's right to not only own slaves but to take them into new territories. His stand was not popular among his fellow senators, and some accused him of treason.

Before Lincoln even took office, the South began its withdrawal from the Union. Though Breckinridge wanted to hold the nation together, he did believe that the states had chosen to form a government in the first place and therefore had the right to choose to dissolve that government. This was not a popular stand either. And when war inevitably erupted, he was forced to leave his Senate seat, leave his home state and leave his old life behind as he sided with the Confederacy. His life would never be the same.

Born on January 16, 1821, John Cabell Breckinridge was the only boy among five sisters in a notable Kentucky family known for its political involvement. Pursuing a career focused on law and eventually politics, John attended several educational facilities and received tutoring from members of Transylvania's fine law department. Though he studied in Lexington, he soon relocated to Iowa to practice law. During a return visit to Lexington, he courted and married Mary Cyrene Burch, who would share the ups and downs of his life, standing by him through the devastating aftermath of the Civil War.

His political career charged forward, taking him quickly into the heart of Kentucky issues, and as James C. Klotter put it in *The Breckinridges of Kentucky*, "Now his future would be tied to Kentucky." By 1849, he was elected to the Kentucky House of Representatives. He moved on from there to the United States House of Representatives, winning the seat that had once been Henry Clay's; he held that position for two terms and then decided not to run again. Keeping occupied with his farm, law practice and as head of the Kentucky Association for the Improvement of the Breed of Horses, John seemed done, at least for the time being, with politics.

However, politics refused to stay away from John C. Breckinridge. As Klotter phrased it, "But politics would not long ignore Breckinridge, nor he it." His party nominated him for vice president of the United States on the ticket with James Buchanon; they ran on the slogan of "Buck and Breck." Campaigning energetically for the ticket, Breckinridge impressed his listeners with his skills as a powerful and moving speaker. Basil W. Duke mentioned in his *Reminiscences*, "His ability as a statesman, his political astuteness, and extraordinary power as an orator were universally recognized and acknowledged." Buck and Breck won the day, and Breckinridge, at only thirty-five, became the youngest vice president the nation had ever elected.

Before his term as vice president of the nation even ended, Breckinridge found himself gaining a United States Senate seat in advance. His popularity in his home state carried him along like a flood tide. Meanwhile, as vice president, he continued to do the job and do it well. Even enemies and opponents noted his fairness and honesty. John C. Breckinridge was on a fast track to success and achievement. Not surprisingly, his name came up quickly during party discussion for the presidential candidate for that 1860 election. Who among the available candidates could beat Lincoln?

That was when the Democratic Party split over states' rights and slavery issues, rupturing any chance of unity within the party. The loss to Lincoln would be Breckinridge's sole political defeat. Though he tried wholeheartedly to unify the party, to draw votes from all sections of the country, he never found a balance that would work. His Southern roots were too strongly established, and he was seen nationally as an advocate for sectionalism. In spite of that reputation, Breckinridge hoped to avoid war and somehow keep the nation together.

Though he had owned slaves, he'd also been influenced by an uncle who served to some extent as a surrogate father when Breckinridge lost his own at a very young age. His uncle, Reverend Robert J. Breckinridge, made a name for himself in emancipationist circles, speaking out, with Henry Clay, for gradual emancipation. Whatever influence this uncle might have had on John when he was a youth, during his political career, John stood foursquare for states' rights and slavery as being a topic off limits to U.S. lawmakers. He saw slavery as an ownership issue rather than a moral/economic/human rights issue. He did not seem interested in grappling with any ambiguities involved between rights to liberty and rights to own people.

Bluegrass Breeding Ground of Power

Lincoln won the 1860 election, and the South began lining up to declare its independence. Breckinridge did what he could to somehow stop the exodus of Southern states from the Union. He strongly supported his own state's efforts at neutrality when war loomed. But nothing helped. In the midst of what looked to be an incredibly brilliant political career, John C. Breckinridge was catapulted out of the political arena entirely, leaving his Senate seat and eventually being forced to flee his home state. The United States Senate later officially expelled him as a traitor. He would never again enter U.S. politics. Instead, he would cast his lot with the Confederacy, shifting from political power to military leadership, being commissioned as a general for the CSA. From that moment until the war's end, John C. Breckinridge would stand by his commitment, whether he yearned for peace or not, whether he suspected he served a lost cause or not, whether he longed for home or not.

This was not Breckinridge's first encounter with war and its effects on soldiers. He'd been a major with the Third Kentucky Volunteers in the war with Mexico, though he'd somehow missed the fighting. As Klotter put it, war had "passed him by"; however, he'd "learned some of the realities of war." He'd seen the misery war could cause—sickness, wounds, death. Again, as Klotter saw it, "John C. Breckinridge had experienced war and would not forget." Those earlier experiences prepared him for some of what he would endure in the War of Rebellion, when he struggled against not only battle injuries but also diseases that decimated troops for both sides.

For much of the war he led what came to be called the Orphan Brigade, his men mostly Kentuckians who could not return to their homes while Kentucky remained strongly under Union control and occupation. Some say the brigade got its name because the men were isolated from their homes and families, being orphans shut off from their home state. Others say the name came from their leader, Breckinridge, who after an especially costly battle, reportedly cried out over the terrible losses, "My poor orphans! My poor orphans!" Yet another idea focuses on their losses among their leaders, with several fallen and beloved leaders in a sense abandoning them, leaving them "fatherless."

Whatever the origin of the name, it stuck, and the men trusted and admired Breckinridge, bonding with him and understanding that he kept their welfare at the forefront of his thoughts. He stayed with them, living as they did, while some leaders sought out greater comforts. He paid attention to their needs, working hard to be sure they had the best food, clothing and other supplies he could manage to scrounge up.

Leading the Orphan Brigade, Breckinridge saw his fair share of battle, fighting in bloody conflicts at Shiloh, Murfreesboro, Chickamauga, Chattanooga and more. Duke, who served with Breckinridge, stated his opinion: "I have always believed that Gen. John C. Breckinridge's capacity as a soldier was not fully appreciated by his Southern countrymen, much as they loved and respected him, and, indeed, by none save those who, serving immediately with or under him, had the best opportunity of correctly estimating it." Duke acknowledged that it was among the men who counted on him in tight moments that his reputation stood strongest, among those whose lives depended on him.

In fact, Duke felt that Breckinridge rose to meet the occasion whenever circumstances got bad. As Duke put it, "Nature seemed to have formed him to deal with emergencies." Furthermore, Duke nailed it down, saying, "He rose to his full stature only in the midst of danger and disaster, and

John C. Breckinridge, CSA.
Courtesy of Library of Congress.

was at his best when the occasion seemed desperate." In addition, Duke had seen Breckinridge in action many times, believing him to have a "rare military aptitude," as well as an "indifference to danger." Going on to detail battle events that revealed Breckinridge's best qualities, Duke observed how strongly he attracted the loyalty and dedication of his men, how he showed "strength of character" and "never exerted his authority harshly."

Eventually, those qualities attracted the attention of his superiors, and he was transferred and given charge over the entire Department of Western Virginia, where he continued to exhibit his natural military wisdom, insights and abilities. Duke and other historians note that Breckinridge demonstrated his true strengths in the Battle of New Market, where he led his forces, including Virginia Military Institute cadets who eagerly volunteered to help, to a decisive victory.

Next in his Confederate military career, Breckinridge found himself reassigned yet again, this time to become the final secretary of war for the CSA, just in time to see the end of the war looming. Among the few tasks left as the Confederacy collapsed, Breckinridge organized the evacuation of the CSA capital, Richmond, Virginia. Seeing to the countless details of a disintegrating government, he gathered paperwork, directed transportation from the city and essentially became the last top government official left in the city before Union forces moved in.

Making certain that the rest of the cabinet, as well as President Jefferson Davis, got safely away from the capital before it fell into Union hands, Breckinridge then headed south himself to rejoin the cabinet. His onerous responsibilities included polling the generals in the field to ascertain the status of Confederate forces, asking for a genuine assessment of chances for further battle. He could see the hopelessness of continued fighting and advised the generals to rapidly make arrangements for surrender. He then had to communicate the disastrous news of complete collapse of the fighting force to a president who still hoped for some sort of last-minute salvation, even after Lee had surrendered at Appomatox.

It was up to Breckinridge to face harsh realities and make the most sensible decisions, doing his very best to prevent any more lives lost in the final days of the war. He set up diversionary movements to deflect pursuit of Jefferson Davis as the Confederate president headed deeper south in an attempt to escape Union pursuit, and then Breckinridge knew it was time to seek safety himself.

Knowing that the Federal government saw him as a traitor to the nation he'd served as vice president and senator, Breckinridge understood that his chances if he were caught would not be good. Fleeing, he headed south, through Florida, writing a letter eventually to one of his sons, describing some of his hardships while downplaying the genuine deadly risks he faced. On one occasion he noted, "At the same moment I observed that Capt. Wood was overboard…and during the whole night the waves ran very high. It seemed to me that she must go under." His escape, even treated lightly, sounded harrowing. Written after the actual escape, the letter (printed in *The Civil War Times Illustrated*) focused on his "adventures," yet reading between the lines, the escape had to have been debilitating as well as disheartening.

Breckinridge described finding friendly faces who offered aid, but he also detailed unbearable heat, swarming mosquitoes that gave the escapees no peace, ticks that burrowed under the skin and nights spent hidden in muddy swamplands. He described an uncomfortably small boat in which he and his companions headed out to sea. He admitted in the letter to his son of the boat, "It seemed a very frail thing to go on the ocean in." In that "frail" craft, before reaching the ocean, they encountered alligators of good size, one in particular being thirteen feet long and hard to kill.

Having to dig to find water that might be drinkable, eating whatever they could find to survive, fighting off mobs of insects and hiding from possible pursuers, the group struggled to keep going. Once on the ocean in their fragile boat, they fought strong winds that kept driving them back toward shore. Between seasickness and heavy waves that nearly capsized their boat, the escape attempt could easily have ended in disaster and death. At last reaching Cuba, their destination, Breckinridge requested prayers and wrote, "I am sure we all felt profoundly grateful for our deliverance."

From Cuba he continued his journey, heading for England. He would remain in exile from the United States for years, knowing that he was a wanted man who might be tried for treason and worse. With members of his family joining him in exile, he prowled through Europe and settled in Canada among a community of Confederate exiles, some of whom would never return to the nation that had been their homeland.

Finally, in 1868, President Andrew Johnson granted an amnesty that included Breckinridge. At last, he could return to Lexington, to Kentucky, to the homeland he'd left so many years before. He chose not to return to politics. He shaped a new life for himself, a quiet and relatively uneventful life. He worked in law and in business, keeping a fairly low profile, though he did denounce the Ku Klux Klan, speaking against its lawless methods.

Breckinridge, who had seemed a rising star in Kentucky and the nation, had dwindled and virtually vanished from the night sky. His promising career no longer held appeal for him. The man who might have been president never recovered from a wound he suffered during the War Between the States. He died after a two-year struggle as a virtual invalid. In an undated letter from the University of Kentucky Special Collection files, Breckinridge's granddaughter Mary Breckinridge Kirkland wrote of the memorial service after his death, "This was a tribute to a brave and honest man."

Chapter 3

Firebrand

Cassius Clay

C assius Marcellus Clay was ready for trouble, but then Cash, as his friends called him, was always ready for trouble. On the brink of setting up an antislavery newspaper in a solidly pro-slavery community, it made perfect sense to get ready for trouble. "Lexington was the very citadel of slavery in Kentucky," according to H. Edward Richardson in *Cassius Marcellus Clay: Firebrand of Freedom*. Cash saw enemies everywhere, which was not necessarily paranoid. For a man who did not mince words, attacked others verbally, wasn't afraid to wade into a physical fight and spoke his mind freely, Cash undoubtedly made enemies as easily as other men grew facial hair.

Knowing that he would be surrounded by enemies the moment he started up his antislavery paper, Cash got ready. He set up his newspaper office in downtown Lexington, and then he reinforced the door and windows to prepare for attacks. He armed the office heavily with pistols, swords and such, added a pair of small but lethal cannons, topped it off with a keg of gunpowder for blowing the place up in case of intruders and made sure to fashion a trapdoor in case his staff needed to make a quick escape. This was a man prepared to fight against slavery, literally. His life hadn't begun that way.

Born into a slaveholding family, he took slavery for granted in his earliest years. He was born to wealth and ease. A cousin of statesman and gradual emancipationist Henry Clay, Cash explained in his *Memoirs* that he began

Young Cassius Clay.
*Courtesy of Library of
Congress.*

to consider the evils of slavery in his younger years, seeing the unfairness of one group of people being owned by another group. As with many Kentucky slaveholders, Cash's family for the most part treated their slaves better than they might be treated elsewhere. Still, a family story reveals a young slave girl and friend of his being assaulted by an overseer. When the girl defended herself, killing her attacker, she was taken to trial and acquitted, but even so, she was sold as punishment and sent to the Deep South, according to Keven McQueen in his *Cassius M. Clay: Freedom's Champion.*

Cash became increasingly aware of the evils of slavery. He would hear his relative Henry Clay speak against the peculiar institution, and the words of Harry of the West stuck with him. Cash heard Reverend Robert J. Breckinridge, also a declared gradual emancipationist, speak. These early influences had to have made an impact on his life as he began formulating his own antislavery stance.

But when the youthful potential emancipationist headed to Transylvania, or Transy, to begin his education, he brought along his body servant, as did most, if not all, of his young classmates. Ironic as it seems now for a future fiery antislavery advocate to bring a slave with him to school, culturally, it was expected and not unusual. What was certainly unusual was that the future firebrand somehow managed to burn the place down. To the ground. Nothing left but ashes. Though Clay did not confess to his culpability until many decades later, it was Cash's body servant, set to blacking Cash's boots in the hallway of the upper-level dormitory, who caused the inferno. The young slave, working by candlelight, fell asleep from exhaustion. The candle burned down and started a blaze that destroyed Transylvania's main building. Cash moved in with family friends, the Robert S. Todds—daughter Mary would later marry Abraham Lincoln.

At Transy, Cash showed special interest in oratory, though he's said to have studied a wide range of subjects. Cash developed an interest in politics while at Transy and Yale, and he spent some time traveling and studying men of greatness and power. He chose to return to Transy to study law and spent some time courting Mary Jane Warfield, who would become his wife. When his father died, Cash inherited the home, some land and the slaves that went with the homeplace. True to his increasing convictions about the evils of slavery, he freed the slaves he could. Some were held in trust for future heirs, and he could not free them. He spent what money he could get his hands on to purchase more slaves and set them free, as well.

During this time, he developed his stance on slavery more fully. He heard William Lloyd Garrison, famed abolitionist, speak, and though Cash felt himself deeply affected, he did not fully agree with Garrison. This man held that slavery must be abolished by whatever means it took, no matter whether those means were legal or not. Cash held that slavery must end but gradually, as Henry Clay proposed, as a process. In addition, Cash felt that freedom for slaves must come within the framework of the United States Constitution, not by any illegal means whatsoever.

Not only did Cash begin to make "a name for himself as a speaker," as David L. Smiley put it in *Lion of White Hall*, but he also entered politics, becoming state representative from his then home, Madison County. He expressed great interest in politics for much of his life, seeing the political arena as an effective means of achieving an end of slavery. He stood up for his relative Henry Clay for a period of time, was seen as a "solid Whig" and spoke out on behalf of candidates he believed would fight slavery with every legal means possible.

But in addition to developing a reputation as a speaker, emancipationist and political figure, Cassius Clay also gained a reputation as a man to be reckoned with who would not back down from a fight and who seemed surrounded by violence. Not that he pursued violence. Rather, violence sought him out. He was ever prepared for it. According to McQueen, "Cassius was involved in a great many fights and duels," and he killed four men during his life, though always in self-defense. McQueen called it part of the "Clay legend."

Constantly prepared for whatever might be headed his way, Cash kept his Bowie knife strapped across his chest in a sheath. He also usually carried a couple of pistols and wasn't afraid to use them. He soon had a reputation for being a dangerous man. On one notable occasion, Cash found himself attacked by a man with a revolver. The man shot Cash point blank, which clearly justified a response. Clay responded with his slashing Bowie knife. The attacker, said possibly to be a paid assassin, did not fare well. His injuries were terrible. As for Cash himself, when his friends inspected him for a wound, they discovered the shot had hit his knife sheath and been deflected; otherwise, he would have died.

It wasn't the first nor would it be the last time Cassius Clay fought for his life, though this time he was charged with attacking the other man and doing severe damage. In court, Henry Clay represented Cash, establishing that Cash only defended himself against the attacker, and the younger Clay was found not guilty. On a different occasion, Cash hustled off to a pro-slavery rally to express his antislavery sentiments. Not surprisingly, a brawl broke out. One man died, and Cash was so desperately injured that the *Lexington Observer & Reporter* printed his death notice, according to McQueen.

Surviving this near-death experience, Cash plunged even deeper into the antislavery battle, deciding to publish his own newspaper in the heart of slave territory, right in downtown Lexington. Cash settled right into offending as many slave owners as he possibly could. As mentioned before, he'd fortified his office for defense. Then he attacked the tough issues head-on, announcing his intentions publicly. On why he started his paper, the *True American*, Cash said, "My object was to use a State and National Constitutional right—the Freedom of the Press—to change our National and State laws, so as, by a legal majority, to abolish slavery."

In his prospectus for the *True American*, Cash wrote:

A number of native Kentuckians, slaveholders and others, propose to publish in the City of Lexington, a paper devoted to gradual and constitutional

Clay's Lexington office. *Courtesy of Barton Battaile Collection, Lexington Public Library.*

emancipation, so as at some definite time to place our State upon the firm, safe and just basis of liberty. The time has come when a large and respectable party, if not a majority of the people, are prepared to take this subject up, and act so as to secure, the end proposed, without injustice to any but with eminent benefit to all.

Cash proposed to publish weekly, charging $2.50 per year, and he lined up a solid base of subscribers, including some from his own state. He promoted that the paper was "Devoted to Universal Liberty; Gradual Emancipation in Kentucky; Literature; Agriculture, Elevation of Labor, Morally and Politically; Commercial Intelligence, etc., etc." He began publishing the *True American* on June 3, 1845, becoming, as McQueen pointed out, "one of the few anti-slavery newspaper editors in the South."

Boldly declaring slavery evil while publishing in the heart of slave country, Cash probably wasn't surprised that death threats began pouring in, nor was he unprepared. When infuriated citizens accused him of fomenting discord and danger in the community, even fearing he might stir up slave rebellion, Cash braced for trouble.

His opponents finally took action in August of the same year, so Cash printed an extra edition to denounce their tactics aimed at destroying his paper. Printing a letter received from Thomas H. Waters, Cash revealed that the citizens of Lexington had resolved that the *True American* must cease. Their committee had decided that Clay must "discontinue the publication of the paper called 'The True American' as its further continuance, in our judgment, is dangerous to the peace of our community, and to the safety of our homes and families."

Cash replied to the letter, which he pointed out that he received "on my sick bed, at my house." He responded with contempt, refused to accept that his paper might stir up problems among the slaves and said to his enemies, "Go tell your secret conclave of cowardly assassins that C.M. Clay knows his rights and how to defend them." But they'd caught him at his weakest moment, suffering from serious illness, vulnerable and barely able to stand up. Desperately, he appealed for aid to his fellow Kentuckians, hoping they would support him in this struggle:

> *Where will you be found when the battle between Liberty and Slavery is to be fought? I cannot, I will not, I dare not question on which side you will be found. If you stand by me like men, our country shall yet be free but if you falter now, I perish with less regret when I remember that the people of my native State, of whom I have been so proud, and whom I have loved so much, are already slaves.*

His appeal failed. Lexington citizens closed down his publishing office, dismantled his equipment and shipped the printing press to Cincinnati. Greatly discouraged but still undaunted, Cash recovered his health and began publishing the *True American* from Cincinnati, writing his editorials in Lexington and behaving as if the paper still originated there in his home city.

Though the paper continued a while longer, Cash found a new avenue for his energy and determination, heading off to fight in the war against Mexico. He set off in search of glory. If he gained a reputation as a bold warrior, perhaps people would pay more attention to his antislavery views. Besides, Cash Clay believed in his country and was willing to fight to defend it. Instead of becoming a battlefield hero, Cash found himself and his men captured by the enemy. Even as a prisoner, Cash proved his mettle, standing up for his men, looking after their needs, keeping them safe and clearly caring about them and their welfare. He gained their respect and loyalty so that, once released, Cash arrived in Lexington and was welcomed as a hero after all.

Establishing a reputation as a national speaker, Cash found numerous opportunities to let the country know his views on slavery, to stand up for what he believed and influence others, including Abraham Lincoln. During a speaking engagement in Springfield, Illinois, in 1854, Cash felt pleased to see his old friend from Lexington, Mary Todd, and her long-legged husband. Mary and Cash's wife, Mary Jane, had been close friends in their youth, and Cash was delighted to renew the friendship. In his later memoirs, Cash would declare that he had "sowed seed" for the future president, who heard Cash speak his mind on the evils of slavery. From then on, Cash considered himself a friend of Lincoln, working for Lincoln's eventual road to the land's highest office.

Pleased when Lincoln gained the presidency, Cash watched as the Union disintegrated and rushed to the capital to lead his own battalion in defending the city and ridding the area of as many Southern sympathizers as he could.

Emancipationist Cassius Clay. *Courtesy of Library of Congress.*

In his memoirs, he explained, "I visited Lincoln often, at the White House, and the Soldier's Home; and left him in much better spirits than when I first arrived in Washington." Cash discussed with Lincoln how he could best serve the president and the nation during a time of war. He chose to represent Union interests in Russia, speaking out on behalf of his country.

On occasions when Cash returned to the United States, he wrote in his memoirs that Lincoln consulted with him about emancipation. Fearing that Kentucky might be lost to the Union if he declared emancipation for slaves, Lincoln asked Cash's opinion, and Cash assured the president that he'd been preaching emancipation and the end to slavery for a quarter of a century, that Kentuckians were no strangers to that viewpoint. He also assured the president that anybody who would leave for the Southern cause had already gone and that Kentucky would stay firm. According to Cash's memoirs, Lincoln then decided to propose the Emancipation Proclamation.

Cash headed back to Russia and continued his efforts to keep Europe from siding with the Confederacy and giving support and aid to the South. Greatly grieved by Lincoln's death, Cash welcomed the war's end, at least, and felt he'd had a strong influence in bringing an end to slavery in the country. He stayed in Russia several more years before returning to his Bluegrass homeland. His long life was never dull, always lively, sometimes violent and filled with controversy. Men still feared Cash Clay, nicknamed the Lion of Whitehall, his homeplace not all that far from Lexington. He never stopped stirring up trouble and being prepared for the results, and he kept large dogs, guns, knives and even cannon handy at all times.

Always ready for a good fight, standing firm for what he believed, edging into what his family declared as insanity, Cassius Marcellus Clay ended life at the age of ninety-two, dying in his own bed. The people he spent his life defending came from miles around to honor him, lining the road for his funeral, showing the world that he would never be forgotten as a man who spoke out for freedom, as a firebrand who would not back down, as a fearless advocate of liberty for all.

Chapter 4

Fugitive Slave

William Wells Brown

S lavery, even in its so-called "mildest form" in Kentucky, offered little hope for men, women and children born into bondage like William. Slaves owned nothing. Not their clothing. Not their homes. Not their families. Not their futures. Slaveholders provided clothing rations, whatever food the owner deemed necessary, housing of often the crudest kind and an unpredictable life. Slave owners decided whether a slave might be allowed to marry, often deciding to whom, when and for how long. Slave marriages had no legal status, since legally speaking slaves were considered property, not citizens.

One day, a particular slave's life might fit into that "milder" category. He might be a household slave, trained for indoor duties, dressed better than most, fed better, allowed relatively free run of the household and be in what seemed a stable family relationship. The next day, life might shift drastically for that slave. If the owner died without a will, leaving behind debts, a slave might be hauled away from home and family to be sold at auction. Many experienced just that sort of sudden, terrible shift in their lives.

So that slave life, no matter how "mild" it might seem to be, was still indisputably bondage. Even in the kindest of households, slaves were often punished for mistakes or disobedience, even if unfairly accused. Beatings occurred regularly for many. Some households provided medical care. Others did not. Some families treated their slaves with respect and kindness. Many did not. There was no set standard because, again, slaves were considered

Slave cabin. *Courtesy of Barton Battaile Collection, Lexington Public Library.*

legally to be property. Nobody had much right to interfere with how a slave owner treated his property.

Not only were slaves beaten with whips, sticks or whatever came to hand, but also they might be punished by being shipped off to the Deep South to work themselves to death as field hands. Fear and uncertainty always hung over even the best treated among slaves. Owning nothing and having no rights, slaves were at the mercy of capricious owners.

Some owners might insist on education for "their" slaves. They might provide religious training as well. Others avoided any education or enrichment of the slaves in their household for fear that an educated slave might resist a life of bondage and helplessness. Slave owners often feared and disliked freedmen, slaves who had bought their freedom or been set free by their masters. Freedmen might bring restlessness or discontent among slaves. Owners did not want their property to get ideas about freedom.

And one of the worst aspects of slavery destroyed any chance of stable family lives. Since slaves were considered property, even their own children did not belong to them. Owners felt justified in selling children away from their mothers as casually as they would sell foals or calves. To make matters

Lexington slave jail. *Courtesy of Barton Battaile Collection, Lexington Public Library.*

worse, slaveholders often fathered those slave children themselves and still felt no compunction about selling their own offspring.

No wonder, then, that William Wells Brown felt no affection for the state or the city where he was born into slavery. His account of his slave experiences opens with the simple statement, "I was born in Lexington, KY." He continued to make his experiences as a slave clear: "The man who stole me as soon as I was born, recorded the births of all the infants which he claimed to be born his property." From the instant of birth, William (his only name at the time) had no rights, even to his own life. As a slave, William learned little of his heritage, knowing only that his mother bore seven children, all with different fathers. Even his own birth date was uncertain.

He would later learn that slaveholders kept slaves in ignorance for their own reasons. For instance, when selling slaves, owners might insist that slaves pretend to be ten years younger than their actual age in order to get a better price for them. And, of course, slave owners did not want slave children realizing that their owners were also their fathers. Though, as William noted, many times the young slave child might be so light complected and bear such a striking resemblance to the owner that visitors would mistake the child for a legitimate family member.

William later based his writings on several such true events where "slaves" as light skinned as any owner found themselves on the auction block, sold off to settle an owner's debts or because a light-skinned slave child looking just like a family member annoyed or shamed the owner's family. Later, after he escaped from the life of bondage he'd been born into, William would begin to tell not only his story but also the stories of individuals he personally knew. His words stirred hearts throughout the nation and overseas as well. He became known as a powerful speaker, a dramatic voice for freedom for every person, no matter what race or background.

In his first published work, his *Narrative*, Brown described his earliest memories as a slave child. The slave owner soon left the Lexington area, and, of course, the slaves went, too. His mother was a field hand, subject to long, harsh working days and also to whippings if she showed up even a few moments late for work. Brown described hearing his mother being beaten for lateness, listening to her cries, hearing "every crack of the whip," knowing she was being desperately hurt and there was nothing he could do to help her. He wept aloud for her and intended to later take her with him on an escape attempt. He could not bear to leave her behind in his bid for freedom.

He'd early decided he would not spend his entire life in bondage. He would not live under the rule of another human being. He longed for freedom with a fierce and abiding hunger. When the master decided to sell off Brown's mother and siblings, he felt helpless and wanted to somehow protect them, especially his sister and mother. He couldn't help his sister, but he did persuade his mother to come with him in an attempt to free themselves.

The effort was grueling and dangerous. They suffered miserably and in the end were captured, taken back and locked away, apart from each other. Brown was able to visit with his mother one more time, and she urged him to keep trying, to go after his liberty. That would be the last time he ever saw her. She was sold south. His inner drive for freedom kept on growing. When a soothsayer promised he'd be free, he wanted to believe.

He'd been "rented out" to work for other masters in several different tasks, ranging from a printing shop to a slave trader's business, which he hated more than any other work he'd been hired out to do. When he next made a try for freedom, he determined to either be free or die. He'd seen other slaves make the same choice, refusing to live their lives in bondage. He'd learned to trust no one, to forage for food to survive and to follow the North Star toward freedom. At last, he found a man he could trust, a man who truly believed every human being had a right to freedom. This man, a Quaker, helped him become a free man at long last, and in honor of this man's kindness, William adopted his rescuer's name, Wells Brown, and added it to his own.

Because he knew slavery and its horrors, Brown dedicated himself to helping other slaves escape. In 1842, while working on a steamboat, he helped sixty-nine fugitive slaves escape into Canada, where they could begin new lives as free persons. He would spend the majority of his life fighting for human rights for slaves, speaking out on their behalf.

His speaking appearances aimed at educating the public to the genuine ugliness of slavery. Many in the North had no actual idea of what slaves experienced. He became widely known and appreciated for his skills as a speaker, but he also developed his writing skills. He would win acclaim as a novelist, playwright and historian, as well as an activist.

William Wells Brown (upper center). *Courtesy of Library of Congress.*

Because of his status as a fugitive slave, his friends became concerned about his safety. Fugitive Slave Laws, effective throughout the nation, made a life of public appearances risky for Brown. His friends and colleagues among abolitionists worried that he would be captured and returned to his former owner. So, Brown wound up overseas, continuing his efforts on behalf of freedom for all men. While in voluntary exile in England, he worked on his novel, the first published by an African American. Published in 1853 in England, his novel proved controversial. He'd based the work on a notorious story about an American political figure who had allegedly fathered children by a slave woman; the specific subject of Brown's book made publication in the United States questionable until he removed references to the American leader and made some other changes.

Titled *Clotel or the President's Daughter*, the novel focused on the abandoned slave woman and her two daughters of mixed race, then labeled as mulatto. Despite their previous circumstances as pampered family members, they found themselves sold at auction. As Brown put it, "Thus closed a Negro sale, at which two daughters of Thomas Jefferson, the writer of the Declaration of American Independence, and one of the presidents of the great republic, were disposed of to the highest bidder!" His point is clear. Throughout the novel, he highlighted hypocrisy and betrayal, showing that slavery created monstrous evils in every direction.

Much of the novel reflects his own experiences and awareness of slave situations. Having worked for a slave trader himself, also known as a "soul seller," Brown revealed atrocities of an almost endless variety in the novel, showing deceit and self-deception among slaveholders. Throughout the work, Brown used some characters as spokespersons, putting abolition speeches in their mouths. For instance, Georgiana, who, as Brown put it, "had learned to feel deeply for the injured Negro," spoke out, "'Thou shalt love thy neighbor as thyself.' This single passage of Scripture should cause us to have respect to the rights of the slave." She worked at persuading others to her viewpoint, just as Brown did.

Brown revealed hypocrisy in religious leaders who taught slaves only as much religion as would make them better slaves. Brown used Georgiana repeatedly to hammer at his points. She said, "Everybody knows that slavery in its best and mildest form is wrong." When she inherited the family slaves, Georgiana worked out a system of gradual emancipation in which the slaves earned the money they'd need to live free lives; she would "prepare the Negro for freedom."

Yet another character, Henry Morton, spoke for Brown as well, saying of the slave, "He has no voice in the laws which govern him. He can hold no property. His very wife and children are not his. His labour is another's. He, and all that appertain to him, are the absolute property of his rulers." Later, yet another character, George, cried out, "What right has one man to the bones, sinews, blood, and nerves of another? Did not God make us all?"

The novel solidly supported Brown's case for an end to slavery. At times heavy-handed in its message, still the novel had been designed for just that purpose. It was often melodramatic, sometimes sentimental, yet many scenes communicated the genuine anguish of the life in bondage that Brown had experienced and wanted others to understand.

During his lifetime, Brown altered portions of that first novel. He also worked on dramas, collections of essays and historic accounts of the Negro in wartime, especially the Civil War. A later work, *My Southern Home or The South and Its People*, took an ironic approach to much of the same material. In this work, Brown poked fun with satire and dark wit. For instance, while discussing the master's religious dedication, Brown wrote, "On Sabbath mornings, reading of the Scriptures, and explaining the same, generally occupied from one to two hours, and often till half of the Negroes present were fast asleep. The white members of the family did not take as kindly to the religious teaching of the doctor, as did the blacks." Another wonderfully satiric segment showed the doctor and his wife hoping for a nice yellow fever or cholera epidemic to improve his business prospects. They needed the area to be "more sickly." They agreed, "We must trust in the Lord. Providence may possibly send some disease among us for our benefit."

Then Brown noted, "Cruelty to Negroes was not practiced in our section." Well, aside from a few necessary floggings and such. And when the reverend's slave ran away, the minister hired dogs to chase down the escapee. Wrote Brown, "The parson and some of the neighbors went along for the fun that was in store." The reverend, of course, was a "humane" fellow and asked that the dogs' owner be careful not to injure the slave if he could help it.

Whether with savagely Mark Twain–like humor or a more direct account of his own struggles, William Wells Brown spoke out on behalf of equality for all men. Though perhaps overshadowed by fellow emancipationist Frederick Douglass, his efforts aided in the search for freedom that Abraham Lincoln would publicly declare in his Emancipation Proclamation.

Chapter 5

Thunderbolt of the Confederacy

John Hunt Morgan

In the dark of night he made his move, giving orders that his men unquestioningly obeyed, as they would for the days, months and years to come while the war raged. He was their captain, and they would follow him, gladly, wherever he took them. He had that kind of power over them. They respected him, gave him their loyalty, committed to follow him right into the thick of the war. John Hunt Morgan had formed their group, the Lexington Rifles, drilled them, marched them and watched over them, and now, having waited as long as they could, it was time to leave; time to leave their homes and families, time to leave their businesses and responsibilities, time to leave Lexington.

Kentucky's efforts to stay neutral had collapsed. The legislature declared for the Union. Lincoln guns had begun to pour into the city to be distributed among Union supporters. Word reached them that Southern sympathizers might be ferreted out and arrested. Certainly, their weapons would be confiscated. Morgan had no intention of allowing that, so he'd decided: time to make their move. He set a small group to marching at the armory, making enough noise to fool everyone into thinking they were all there. He'd smuggled their guns under loads of hay in wagons that would move out with them. Then he led his men out of the city under cover of darkness.

None of them wanted to leave. None wanted to say farewell to friends and family. None wanted to leave their homes or the city of Lexington. None wanted to say farewell to the state they loved. But Kentucky had chosen to stick with the Union, at least for the moment. Morgan believed in his heart that given time and persuasion, Kentucky would go with its Southern roots. He never stopped believing that somehow, eventually, Kentucky would join with the Southern cause. Leaving Lexington that night with his men, Morgan likely expected to be back soon, with plenty of troops at his back and with an assurance that Lexington and all of Kentucky would welcome him and the Confederacy with wholehearted devotion.

Though he'd been born in Huntsville, Alabama, John Morgan loved his adopted home state. His family lived there, and he was always a person committed to family. He'd spent most of his youth in or near Lexington. It was home for him, for his mother, Henrietta, whom he adored, for his two sisters and his five brothers, who would all eventually fight with him. In his Lexington youth, John was popular. He had close friends and enjoyed an active life. Not much for classroom studies, still he attended Transylvania, which was to be expected of well-bred young Southern men.

When he got into trouble at Transylvania and was suspended, John evidently felt he'd had enough of education and was ready to move on, which he did. When the war with Mexico began, he headed out to tackle a life of action and adventure. Chosen an officer, he didn't see much in the way of action but did get his first taste of military life and felt drawn to it. Once he returned to Lexington, though, he settled into a regular life of success in business, partnering with Sanders Bruce and marrying his partner's sister Rebecca Bruce. He also partnered with his brothers, running a hemp factory and buying slaves to work the factory and also to hire out as laborers for other businesses.

Though his wife, Rebecca, proved frail, losing their baby and becoming an invalid, generally life treated him well. His business ventures prospered, and he found himself not only successful but a community leader as well, involved as captain of the volunteer fire company, member of the school board, a Mason, organizing local militia group the Lexington Rifles and donating funds to Transylvania. He made his sentiments clear concerning the national division by boldly flying a Confederate flag over his hemp factory.

As war loomed over the state, John Morgan waited. When those Lincoln guns showed up, Morgan and his militiamen gathered nearby, ready to defend themselves against armed Union supporters. Lexington came disturbingly close to armed warfare in the city streets that day as both sides readied for a fight. Only the quick intervention of men like Senator John C. Breckinridge saved the city from bloodshed. Breckinridge urged the militia to step back and stay calm. The time for fighting would come, but not yet.

When Morgan's invalid wife died, he felt free to step out into the gathering storm of battle, taking his militia with him. They headed out of town in search of the Confederate forces and immediately offered their services, eager to join the fight. With his friend and second in command, Basil W. Duke, by his side, John Hunt Morgan set out to make a name for himself and for his men, establishing them as raiders without peer. He and his men soon mastered the hit-and-run raid, dashing in among the enemy, usually by night, gathering essential information, taking out unwary pickets and generally making a nuisance of themselves.

That became Morgan's specialty, those flash raids that kept the enemy always on guard, always off balance, always uncertain what he was up to next. Nobody ever knew for sure where John Hunt Morgan and his men would show up. Audacious and unpredictable, Morgan kept everyone on edge, including at times his superior officers, who weren't sure where he

Thunderbolt of the Confederacy, John Morgan. *Courtesy of Library of Congress.*

was either. A master at misdirection and generating rumors, Morgan built a reputation of being everywhere at once. Rumors flew when Morgan hit the area. Wild stories, reports of sightings and incredible exaggerations of his troop strength spread whenever he turned up.

As Duke wrote of Morgan in his *History of Morgan's Raiders*, "he seemed ubiquitous," and Duke added, "He knew how to thoroughly confuse and deceive an enemy." That's what Morgan did best—sow confusion and chaos among the enemy. He delighted in wearing a Union blue coat, showing up here and there, conversing with Union supporters, letting them think he was a Federal soldier and then revealing himself to be the notorious John Hunt Morgan. At times, he would fool and confuse enemy soldiers into believing he was their superior officer; in that way, he rounded up huge groups of prisoners, far more than his men could handle. He'd parole them, getting their promise that they would not rejoin the fighting until they were exchanged for Confederate prisoners.

Morgan always seemed to enormously enjoy taunting and mocking his enemy. He might sit beside someone on a train, start up a conversation about that "rascal Morgan" and then warn his new acquaintance to be on the lookout, since no one ever knew when the wily raider would show up. His men often slipped in among the Union forces to gather information, sometimes wearing civilian clothing, sometimes passing as Union soldiers. Who knows how many times Morgan might have slipped through the cracks to show up at his mother's home in Lexington. That was just the sort of escapade he would enjoy.

His strength and greatest skill clearly came during those raids. Morgan and his men crept into enemy-held territories, disrupting supply lines, burning bridges, tearing up train tracks, destroying train cars and stealing supplies headed for Union troops. He further delighted in playing with telegraph messages, sending false reports, spreading bizarre stories and exaggerating Confederate troop numbers. Disrupting supply lines and slowing down the enemy's plans kept him and his men busily occupied for much of the war.

With Duke by his side, helping to get the men in good tactical shape, Morgan led raids throughout Kentucky, striking here and there, never with any warning, always with plenty of confusion about where he would be and how many men rode with him. He polished the skill of taking his men into dangerous areas, dismounting them to fight and then mounting them to move on again. Union commanders frequently decided to avoid direct confrontation, believing his troop strength to be greater than it usually was.

Because of those hit-and-run raids, he was best known as the "Thunderbolt of the Confederacy," a name he earned time after time. His enemies, however, called him a highwayman or, better yet, the "King of Horse Thieves." Morgan also specialized in either covering a retreat for the Confederacy or keeping the enemy moving along as they retreated. As Duke put it, "He could actively and efficiently harass a retreating army." Duke, who clearly admired his friend and leader, wrote of Morgan, "He was born to be great in the career in which he was so successful." Furthermore, Duke declared that Morgan had "a genius for command," as well as "a quickness of perception and of thought, amounting almost to intuition," and "audacity and wily skill."

Perhaps the finest moment in Morgan's career as a Confederate raider came when he helped persuade high command that Lexington, in the heart of the Bluegrass, and all of Kentucky needed only a slight nudge to plunge wholeheartedly into the Confederacy. Spurred by Morgan's certainty of his home state's Southern leanings, the Confederacy marched into Lexington in September 1862, greeted with cheers and excitement. General Kirby Smith led his troops into a city that flew Confederate flags, waved banners and provided gala feasts. Truly, Lexington appeared ripe to become part of the CSA.

Actually, some Southern sympathizers had already declared Kentucky part of the Confederacy in 1861, choosing a governor, George Johnson, a Transylvania graduate with three degrees, who soon died in battle, to be followed by Richard Hawes, a governor in exile since Union troops drove out the provisional government.

If the welcome encouraged Kirby Smith that Kentucky would declare for the South, Lexington's enthusiasm for Morgan and his men parading through downtown must have provided Morgan's proudest moment. The triumph didn't last long, though. The Confederate occupation of Lexington ended only a few weeks later, and not many Kentuckians rallied to the cause. Most Southern stalwarts had already volunteered. The city settled in for a Union occupation that lasted through the war and beyond.

Morgan never gave up completely on his dream of a staunchly Confederate Kentucky, and he managed to squeeze in a quick dash into

Lexington environs to skirmish with Federal troops billeted on the grounds of the late Henry Clay's estate, Ashland. The raid succeeded, as did many Morgan raids, bringing chaos and confusion to the enemy ranks. As Duke pointed out, Morgan kept on surprising friend and foe alike.

No one would know Morgan better than Duke, who was not only his right-hand man and friend, but also his brother-in-law, marrying Morgan's sister Henrietta, known as Tommie. Duke tried to be as fair and honest as possible about his leader, but his unswerving loyalty and deep admiration show through every word he wrote in what he admitted was an effort to assure Morgan's reputation for posterity. For much of the war, Duke was close by whenever Morgan made decisions, led raids or decided whether or not to obey orders from above, which did not always fall in line with his own ideas.

At times they were separated, though, and Duke could only speculate on those times when they were not fighting side by side. During the Great Raid, when Morgan disobeyed orders and led his men across the river into solidly enemy territory, Duke was not with him the entire time. The raid was bold, unexpected and kept the townspeople in his path agitated and near hysterics over the dreaded Morgan and his men. When they heard Morgan was on his way, locals immediately hid their horses. Everyone knew Morgan liked good horseflesh and usually took what he and his men needed.

Morgan pushed his men hard, but they followed him without question. He had a way with his men. They trusted him. He took them on up through Indiana, into the heart of Union land, taking the war right to the enemy's people. The daring was great. The cost was high, with many of his men killed, wounded or taken captive. Morgan himself would be taken before the raid ended once into Ohio, though not without many typical Morgan antics.

His raiders fought local militias, looted stores, raided for fresh horses and generally made trouble for everyone. When finally cornered, faced with Union forces well beyond anything they could handle, exhausted, hungry, their horses weakened by hard riding, it looked like the end. So Morgan sent out men under a flag of truce. Was the famous John Hunt Morgan getting ready to surrender? Not exactly. Instead, he sent word to the Union commander, insisting that the Union troops surrender to him.

His pursuers knew better. They'd heard about Morgan's skill at bluffing. Demanding his immediate surrender instead, they moved in, only to discover many of his men so exhausted that they'd essentially toppled from their horses sound asleep. Rounded up, wakened, their loaded guns discharged harmlessly into the air, the men were hauled off as prisoners of war. Morgan himself was sent, along with many of his officers, to a penitentiary in Ohio.

Prison bars couldn't hold John Morgan for long, though. His restless nature couldn't well tolerate being inactive while war still raged beyond those bars. As legend has it, one of his officers, Tom Hines, devised an escape plan to dig through the floor, reach a ventilation system and tunnel their way to freedom. Morgan and several of his officers left the prison, made good their escape and never looked back. He wasn't a man meant for prison life.

But with most of his men gone, most of his officers still behind bars and not much left of his old command, Morgan searched for new directions. He'd made some major changes in his life, courting and marrying Miss Martha Ready of Murfreesboro, Tennessee. They made a perfect couple. He wooed her by bringing gifts—Union prisoners. She adored the gifts and the man who brought them. Some would later claim that marriage, especially a happy, successful marriage, did not agree with Morgan, that he lost the edge that made him so good at what he did. Others would say he'd lost some of his drive, some of that dogged determination and boldness that enabled him to succeed where lesser men might have failed. Still others point mainly to the absence of his brother-in-law, still incarcerated and therefore not present to help Morgan lead.

Whatever the case, he got careless. With new troops, men who did not know him as well, who had not been with him all along, the raiding deteriorated into a near crime spree, with looting, bank robberies and such. The Confederate command started an investigation. Morgan ignored them and their orders. He moved out, taking his men on yet another raid. He spent the night in comfort in a home with no guards outdoors in the rain, virtually no sentries and basically no spies to be sure he got accurate information. He also postponed his planned early morning departure, setting himself up for disaster. And that's what arrived, in the form of Union soldiers surrounding the house where he slept that morning.

The story of Morgan's last hours isn't clear. Though friend and comrade Basil Duke later tried to uncover the truth, no one is exactly certain what happened. Some say Morgan tried to sneak out through the garden. Some say he surrendered. Some say women he trusted betrayed him. Whatever the case, John Hunt Morgan was shot and killed on September 4, 1864, in Greeneville, Tennessee, ending the career of the man the Southern people looked to for heroic victories.

He'd established himself as bigger than life, and his death hit the South hard. They'd lost their hero, their hope for the future, their Rebel raider.

Chapter 6

Right-Hand Man

Basil Duke

In a single heartbeat, the man he most admired in the whole world ceased to exist, and for Basil Wilson Duke, the war changed permanently. Duke put it this way in his *History of Morgan's Raiders*: "When he [Morgan] died, the glory and chivalry seemed gone from the struggle, and it became a tedious routine, enjoined by duty, and sustained only by sentiments of pride and hatred." When John Hunt Morgan, Duke's friend, commander and brother-in-law, died, it seemed to signal the end of the Southern cause.

Morgan acted invincible, a man larger than life, a man of uncanny instincts and luck beyond the norm. He rode through life with dash and verve, bold and assertive, enjoying himself when he played pranks on the enemy, somehow always managing to slip through virtually unscathed no matter how tight a scrape he got himself into. Clearly visible in everything Duke wrote about Morgan, the man drew followers to himself, not least among them his second in command, Duke.

Perhaps it was nearly impossible to believe that the Thunderbolt of the Confederacy had actually died. No one who followed his adventures by rumor and hearsay wanted to accept the dire news. Certainly Duke did not. Evidently feeling at a tremendous loss without his friend and leader, Duke traveled to the place Morgan had died to try to find the truth for himself. How could this have happened? How could a man who'd escaped every threat and danger throughout the war so suddenly have reached the end of the magic?

Nobody was clear on what had happened. It seemed so ordinary. He'd been sleeping in, apparently, rather than gathering his men to leave earlier. He'd been in bed when Union troops showed up, surrounding the house where he slept. The story gets murky at this point, and Duke set himself to ferret out the truth of it. As Duke noted, "His fate, however, is still involved in mystery." Stripped down to bare facts, Morgan left the house, whether to flee or to surrender isn't certain, but shortly after, he was shot in the garden.

Had he been betrayed? Had he surrendered and been shot dead anyway? Had his body been mistreated, his corpse paraded around while his enemies celebrated? Whatever the case, John Hunt Morgan was dead. No doubt or confusion about that. He was gone, and for his friends and family, the world had become a much darker place because of that death. Duke, among them all, mourned his loss and felt the devastation of emptiness. "But not only was the light of genius extinguished then, and a heroic spirit lost to earth—as kindly and as noble a heart as was ever warmed by the constant presence of generous emotions was stilled by a ruffian's bullet," Duke wrote. He could not accept "that so much life had been quenched."

Duke could not stop thinking about his beloved leader, writing, "Every trait of the man we almost worshiped, recollections of incidents which showed his superb nature, crowd now, as they crowded then, upon the mind." He added, "Surely men never grieved for a leader as Morgan's men sorrowed for him." Whether the rest of Morgan's men grieved as thoroughly for him or not, certainly Duke found himself devastated with grief. He'd lost the man who stood above all others in his life. He'd lost his wife's well-loved brother, his most trusted friend and the leader for whom he would have willingly died.

Nothing would ever be the same in Basil W. Duke's life, but he never lost the love and commitment he held in his heart for his homeland, for Kentucky and for the South. Duke had been born in Kentucky, in the center of the Bluegrass region, an only child, part of an otherwise large family. He had a pack of cousins. Though his father died when he was young, Duke had plenty of supportive family around and grew up as a Southern gentleman with an ingrained code of honor, an interest in law and politics and a love of fine horseflesh. Not much of a scholar, he still managed to attend several educational institutions, where he did not exactly shine. Though records aren't available, he is said to have graduated from Transylvania's law department.

He headed to Missouri to practice law, but he soon found himself back in Lexington, drawn by the attractions of his future wife, Henrietta Morgan, known to friends and family as Tommie. They wed in 1861 and would spend close to fifty years as husband and wife, through war and whatever else life brought to them. He seemed more drawn to politics than to law and even more so drawn to military interests, getting involved in a militia group in St. Louis. When the war began, Duke was right in the thick of it, volunteering his services, leading scouting expeditions and working out a system of hit-and-run maneuvers that would later show up vividly in Morgan's style of leadership.

Once Kentucky's neutrality effort collapsed and Morgan began his active warfare, Duke connected with Morgan. As Gary Robert Matthews wrote in *Basil Wilson Duke, CSA: The Right Man in the Right Place*, "Thus began a partnership between Morgan and Duke that lasted for almost two years." The partnership would break apart only as Duke suffered serious injuries and was sidelined or when he found himself in a prison for more than a year. But when those two fought together, they made a perfect partnership.

Nobody can quite say for sure which man was most responsible for the success of the partnership. Some historians believe Duke to be the "brains" behind Morgan's men. Others, Duke included, insist that Morgan developed unique and solidly successful battle schemes. When researchers describe Duke as a modest man, that's a gross understatement. Throughout his book on Morgan and his men, Duke rarely had much to say for himself. He frequently and lavishly praised his leader, other officers, the gallant men with whom he served and even those among the enemy who fought well.

Duke's modesty communicates through his writing as clearly as his near-adulation for John Morgan. He literally could not say enough about Morgan. In point of fact, he explained his motives for writing *History* as his effort to assure Morgan's legacy, to defend Morgan against anyone who attacked the leader's greatness and as a detailed justification of Morgan's decisions and actions. Furthermore, Duke spoke from firsthand experience. He was there when Morgan made those decisions. He stood by Morgan's side through much of the war, as advisor and supporter. Duke handled discipline among the troops, a skill Morgan never cared to develop. Duke took care of training the men, preparing them for battle, whipping them into shape and enforcing whatever orders Morgan handed down.

Perhaps Duke provided ideas as well, but without a doubt, Morgan had a way with his men. He knew them and knew how to handle them, at least up until those waning days before his death when his command fell apart. Morgan also had excellent instincts for fighting. Duke detailed how Morgan could tell when informers spoke truth or not, when terrain that he'd never seen before felt familiar to him, when he somehow could put himself in the enemy's shoes and when he could almost read minds as he planned what to do next.

If much of Duke's story seems to focus on Morgan, that is because that's where Duke's commitment stood. Twice injured, Duke missed chunks of the fighting, picking up details for his book from others who were there. Once injured at Shiloh and again later during the famous Christmas Raid, Duke might have died either time. The second injury was described in *One of Morgan's Men* when John M. Porter wrote, "Colonel Duke was seriously, and, it was thought at the time, fatally wounded…Before the nature of his wound was ascertained, and when all of us thought he was killed, I never saw as much sorrow among the men."

Though too modest to let slip the fact that he was also greatly respected and admired by the men, Duke seemed almost obsessed with making sure that his hero, John Morgan, would live in legend way beyond the war. He succeeded. John Morgan's legend stayed alive and well primarily through Duke's exhaustive efforts and devotion. Duke and his wife, Morgan's sister, even named one of their daughters after the fallen commander. They called her Reb for short.

Nothing would ever be the same for Duke, but with a strong sense of duty despite the emotional devastation he experienced, he stepped up to do what had to be done. The men became his once Morgan was gone. Duke's men fought on throughout the war, right up to the very bitter and dark end in the final days of the Confederacy. They served the cabinet and president while the Southern government disintegrated, while Richmond was abandoned and while Southern armies one by one surrendered. Duke even found himself assigned to guard and protect the remains of the Confederate treasury, a task he had absolutely no liking for and felt relieved to be done with.

Duke helped in efforts to assist the cabinet and President Davis to escape as the end drew closer. Then finally, there was no duty left, no war to fight, no Confederacy to support. He went home to his wife and family, to the state

Flight of Jefferson Davis. *Courtesy of Library of Congress.*

he loved. He and his family settled in Louisville, and he worked at making a career for himself, getting involved in the law and politics, becoming the major representative for the Louisville & Nashville (L&N) Railroad—the very same railroad that Morgan's men specialized in destroying, burning bridges, demolishing railroad cars, blowing up depots, raiding supplies and causing as much havoc and difficulty as possible. Their job during the war was often to be as obstructive to the enemy as they could. Destroying L&N Railroad facilities broke up supply and communication lines.

He became known as a skilled speaker, much in demand, especially among historians of the Southern "Lost Cause." He wrote often and well, becoming a magazine editor as well. Duke even met and befriended Teddy Roosevelt. The two men shared a tremendous energy, an interest in history and an enjoyment of a life of action and adventure.

Duke lost his beloved Tommie on October 20, 1909, when she simply slipped away in her sleep with no warning. Devastated by yet another major loss in his life, still Duke carried on with whatever duties lay before him. Keeping alive the memory of John Morgan continued to be a highlight for

Basil W. Duke. *Courtesy of J. Winston Coleman Jr. Photographic Collection, Transylvania University.*

him, as he presided over a massive memorial event in Lexington in 1911: the unveiling of a statue to commemorate Morgan's role in the Civil War. The turnout was astounding—perhaps as many as twenty thousand came to honor the fallen hero.

Duke died quietly on September 16, 1916, and some say that Teddy Roosevelt managed to sneak in for a final visit with his friend before the end. Through his long and productive life, he did the job, whatever that job might be. He fought to the best of his ability when he believed it was right to fight. He supported his commander even beyond death, writing an account of Morgan's exploits that would go far toward keeping the man and the legend as part of posterity. He wrote as much truth as he possibly could, gathering other witness accounts to back up his own memories and experiences. He nurtured a strong sense of history and the value of keeping it relevant.

Basil Wilson Duke never had much to say about himself, preferring to honor others with his words. Inadvertently, he made a name for himself while striving to keep alive the names of others who had done their duty, fought what they believed to be the good fight and served to the best of their ability. Duke believed in the cause he fought for; he believed in Kentucky and Kentuckians. As he wrote at the end of his book on Morgan's men, "They had done their part and served faithfully, until there was no longer a cause and a country to serve." Furthermore, he added, "They knew not what their fate would be, and indulged in no speculation regarding it. They had been taught fortitude by the past, and, without useless repining and unmanly fear, they faced the future." The same could be said for Basil Wilson Duke.

Chapter 7

Undefeated

Joseph Shelby

The war was over. The Confederacy was disintegrating moment by moment. Richmond had fallen. Lee had surrendered. President Jefferson Davis and his cabinet evacuated the capital and moved steadily southward, pursued by Union forces. Davis and a number of Confederate agents had a bounty on their heads. Things did not look good. Joseph Orville Shelby had a decision to make. To surrender or not to surrender. Everyone else apparently had lined up to make their surrender official.

Not Shelby. The decision did not take long to make. Daniel O'Flaherty, in his book *General Jo Shelby: Undefeated Rebel*, quoted Shelby as saying, "Surrender is a word which neither my division nor myself understand." O'Flaherty further quoted Shelby as saying, "To talk of surrender is to be a traitor. Let us seize the traitors and attack the enemy. Forward, for the South and Liberty!" Shelby was committed to the Confederacy. Only one problem: there was no longer a Confederacy.

With the government shattered and fleeing, Richmond fallen and the Confederate forces laying down arms to go home, Shelby stood alone. He and his men had no country to fight for, but why should that stop them? Shelby and his men, known as the Iron Brigade, decided to head south, and by that they meant very south. They would march on into Mexico, offer their services as a mercenary army willing to fight on behalf of the Emperor Maximilian and quietly establish a new Southern nation there in Mexico.

So Shelby and those of his men who chose to join him set off through Texas, making it their business to keep law and order along the way and gathering stray former Confederate soldiers who preferred Mexico to a beaten South. By the time they reached the Mexican border, Shelby had accumulated roughly one thousand men. Getting to the emperor wasn't an easy task. They faced numerous setbacks and problems along the way, but they were undaunted as well as undefeated. So distinctive was their saga that a motion picture based (loosely) on their exploits hit theaters in modern days, starring John Wayne and Rock Hudson.

Though their trek to find and fight on behalf of the emperor did not meet with success—he turned down their generous offer to serve as his personal army—Shelby's men made history with their choice to refuse to surrender. Shelby stood firm in his decision. He would not seek pardon or admit defeat. He'd come from a proud and noble family, and that was his way of standing up for what he believed.

The Shelby name was a notable one in Kentucky, where Jo was born and raised. His family had produced the first Kentucky governor, Isaac Shelby, and continued producing men of worth and value to the state. Kentucky was his homeplace, as it was for so many notable men in the Civil War era. His father died when he was young, and his mother took him back to her family in Lexington, Kentucky. When she remarried widower Benjamin Gratz, Jo acquired a stepfather and assorted stepbrothers who would be some of his childhood companions.

Not only did Jo enjoy the company of the Gratz boys, but also he soon made staunch friends in Lexington, such as John Hunt Morgan, Benjamin Gratz Brown and Frank Blair Jr. Jo attended Transylvania, as did so many of the young men of the time, though like his buddy John Morgan, Jo wasn't much of a scholar. Both Jo and John Morgan enjoyed pranks more than studies, getting themselves into trouble here and there. Later, both men would follow similar careers in the Confederacy, leading cavalry units, outwitting the enemy and coming up with interesting and innovative methods of pursuing warfare.

Both Morgan and Shelby enjoyed physical activities. Both especially delighted in riding fine horses, and both had an eye for superb horseflesh, which aided them later in wartime when they sought reliable horses for themselves and their men. Shelby and Morgan also both grew up accustomed to slavery. Jo's mother bought a young slave at the Lexington slave market to be his companion and servant. Billy Hunter, the same age as Shelby at the time, eleven years old, spent most of his life serving Jo. Even after he'd gained his freedom, Billy Hunter returned to being Jo's companion and friend.

Jo and his friends in Lexington, Kentucky, lived a boisterous and adventurous life, taking part in sports, hunting and other manly activities, though they enjoyed spending time with the ladies as well. Those friendships between Jo and the young men he knew in Lexington would survive even severe differences during the war. Frank Blair Jr., who stayed at the Gratz house while studying at Transylvania, would go on to support Lincoln for president, fight for the Union, help keep the state of Missouri from seceding and later be a vice presidential candidate running against Grant. Gratz Brown would fight for the Union, be elected a Missouri governor, serve in the Senate and run for vice president with Horace Greeley.

Jo's friends and family members stood so strongly for the Union that Frank Blair Jr.'s brother Montgomery became Lincoln's postmaster general,

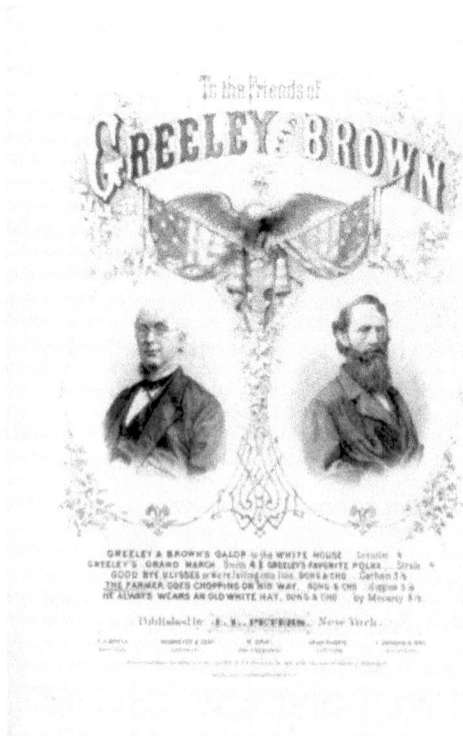

Greeley and Brown campaign poster. *Courtesy of Library of Congress.*

General Frank P. Blair. *Courtesy of Library of Congress.*

a cabinet position. His illustrious career covered a wide spectrum, including studying law at Transylvania and becoming attorney for Dred Scott in the famous Supreme Court case. The Blair family had made its mark on the nation all along with the boys' father, Frank Blair Sr., graduating from Transylvania, serving on President Jackson's "kitchen cabinet," becoming an influential journalist and editor for the *Washington Globe* and establishing a home in Washington that would eventually become Blair House, home to vice presidents. The elder Blair had declared himself antislavery. Though he owned slaves, he would later tell them they could leave at any time and be free, though most chose to stay.

Oddly, then, Shelby's oldest and strongest friendships developed with young men and their families who would stand with the Union. Jo's stepfather, Benjamin Gratz, was a solid Union man, as were his sons. Surrounded by pro-Union men, still Jo chose his own path and followed the Southern cause, becoming more or less an outcast among the family back home. Before the war broke out, Jo had relocated to Missouri, along with several of his friends. Shelby and one of his stepbrothers started a business together, and he pursued a variety of business ventures, seeming successful for the most part before the war. He'd studied his stepfather's hemp business from end to end and had prepared himself for a promising future before war intervened.

War hit hard and fast in Jo Shelby's world. He'd settled in Missouri, made a success of his business ventures and even found the right young woman, Betty, to marry and started a family. Still, when war found him, he stepped forward ready to meet it. He walked away from home, family, businesses and farming ventures, which included fine horses. He gathered recruits and fought to keep Missouri free from what he considered government oppression. Without any real formal military training, Jo apparently had a gift for leadership and battlefield insight, just as did his childhood friend John Morgan. And like Morgan, Jo Shelby knew how to handle his men. He took care of them, keeping them as well equipped as he possibly could.

Jo never spared those men, though, or himself. A demanding leader, he pushed himself and his soldiers hard. He devised schemes for unusual techniques, always knowing somehow when to keep his men on horseback and when to get their feet on the ground to fight. He devised a system for covering a retreat that involved dividing his men into small companies, setting them short distances apart and establishing a sort of relay technique, where the men shot and then fell back, allowing the next group to shoot and then fall back and reload. As with Morgan, nobody knew how many men he had or where they were. And again, as with Morgan, Jo Shelby's men often wore enemy uniforms, which sometimes got them shot if captured.

Also like his friend Morgan, Shelby did not feel at ease sitting around camp. He required action, even if it was going out to recruit more troops, which he did with substantial success. When he recruited men, they stayed recruited, willing to follow him wherever he took them. He inspired loyalty in his men, as did Morgan. Both men were known for their long-distance raids and their skill at anticipating the enemy's plans.

In his book *Cavalry Raids of the Civil War*, Colonel Robert W. Black said of Shelby, "Wherever there was a fight, Joe Shelby seemed to be in it and he quickly rose in rank." Black went on to note, "Shelby was happiest when raiding." In one raid, Black pointed out that Shelby destroyed five Union forts, killed or captured hundreds of men, tore up railroads and added to his men's supplies from Union stores. Again, Jo sounds a lot like his childhood pal John Morgan. Neither man was formally trained, and both men held a natural talent for warfare.

Shelby's name was known and feared, but it was also respected by the men who faced him on the battlefield. His enemies knew he was a man to be reckoned with, but they also saw him as a commander of honor and fairness. When he fought, he put everything into it, fighting with what Black called "vigor." On one battlefield, he faced one of his stepbrothers, Cary Gratz, though whether Shelby knew it at the time isn't certain. Shelby survived the conflict that day. Cary Gratz did not, dying from his wounds on the field, and was sent home to Lexington for burial in the Lexington Cemetery. Jo had chosen to go on a different path from his brothers and cousins.

Still, when times got rough, the family was there for him. When the fighting went badly in Missouri and Jo's wife and children needed a refuge, he got in touch with friends and family back in Kentucky. His stepfather, Benjamin Gratz, came personally to bring Jo's wife and children back to Lexington for safe refuge. More than once in his tumultuous lifetime, Jo counted on those family ties.

Despite Jo Shelby's tenacious efforts, the war faltered in Missouri. Jo gave it everything he had, refusing to quit on the Confederacy, but it didn't look good. More than once Jo fought until his horse was shot right out from under him. In one battle, he lost three or four horses during the fighting, yet he survived. And once, on the brink of being captured, Jo was saved by none other than Frank James, later to be known as one of the James Boys, notorious train robbers and elusive bandits.

Deeply loyal, Jo Shelby never forgot that debt to Frank James. In later life, Jo welcomed both James brothers, Frank and Jesse, into his home, even allowing Frank to stay with his family during a lengthy illness. Later still, Jo Shelby spoke at the trial of Frank James as a character witness and helped get Frank acquitted. Jo never turned his back on someone who had helped him.

Once the war seemed doomed to failure, Jo Shelby considered his options, made his decision never to surrender, worked out his big plans for Mexico and a new Confederacy and set to making those plans a reality. Though the Mexico experiment failed, Shelby gave it his best effort. The emperor had granted land to Shelby and those of his men who chose to stay; however, the land was not the emperor's to give. When conflict in Mexico escalated, the

Rebels in voluntary exile faced battle yet again, but this time they'd brought their families with them, expecting to settle permanently in Mexico. Jo and those of his followers who survived the heated conflict faced facts: there was no new Confederacy for them in Mexico.

Heading back at long last to the United States, Jo and his family headed to Lexington, Kentucky, but only for a visit. Home had become Missouri, and the Shelby family wanted to head home. Though they'd lost the house, burned to the ground, they were determined to start over again. Jo Shelby had a heart for farming, raising crops and livestock, so he pursued that course, searching out business opportunities as well. He found himself in politics but behind the scenes, refusing to trade on his war reputation and popularity to gain a political seat.

The Shelby family kept more or less an open house, with the James brothers, Cole Younger and such lawbreakers as welcome as any of Jo's former men from the Iron Brigade. Jo was well liked, and his men sought him out for help, advice and friendship. His family continued to grow. Like Duke, he became a railroad executive, which was ironic since both were commanders whose men had happily destroyed railroads and railroad property during the war. Plus, of course, he befriended men who made a career of robbing railroads.

Eventually, Jo Shelby became a United States marshal for western Missouri, which again seemed somewhat ironic. His enemies protested, saying he'd been a lawless man himself for many years, which wasn't exactly fair, since it was in wartime, but they had a more valid protest about the company he kept with bandits and robbers like Frank James. Shelby got the job and did his best, as he always did. He hired deputies and welcomed old soldiers to hang out with him. His former slave, Billy Hunter, found his way back to be at Shelby's side.

When Jo developed an annoying cold, disliking any form of illness, he kept on working until the cold developed into pneumonia, which quickly worsened. His death brought sorrow among the many who admired and respected him. He stood up for what he believed. He didn't do things by half measures, and he stuck with his friends no matter what anybody else said or thought. He was a man of his word. The state of Missouri grieved his loss. He was buried with honors there at Forest Hill Cemetery, attended by his Iron Brigade men and Billy Hunter, who led a riderless horse.

Though his reputation might have been tarnished for some by his continued association with men like the James brothers, Jo Shelby stepped into history as a legend of sorts. He followed his own heart, stayed on the path he believed right and refused to surrender. He went down in history as the Confederate who never gave up the Lost Cause, as the undefeated, the man who kept his commitment regardless of what anyone else chose to do.

Chapter 8

Families Divided

The war that shattered the Union literally divided families, pitting brother against brother, friend against friend, neighbor against neighbor. Nowhere was this more clearly evident than in Kentucky and Lexington, where the nature of this "brothers' war" ripped through the notable families of the day. From the highest levels of power and authority to the level of ordinary citizens, the war tore apart relationships. The painful divisiveness of the War of the Rebellion even reached the president of the United States, struggling to hold the Union together, to mend the brokenness. Lincoln's Confederate in-laws brought grief and sorrow right into the White House.

When Lincoln married Mary Todd of Lexington, Kentucky, he soon found himself with relatives who were accustomed to slaveholding and who were thoroughly Southern in their attitudes and orientations. It must not have surprised the Lincolns when a large portion of Mary's family went strongly for the South when war took hold of the nation. Mary's family divided almost exclusively along the lines of her father's first wife's children opposed to those children of the second marriage. Mary's full sisters had moved north to Illinois, finding husbands there, and those family members stood with the Union.

Of Mary's brothers, one sided with the Confederacy, along with her half sisters and their husbands, as well as her half brothers. Mary's half brothers Samuel and Alexander both died fighting for the Confederacy, as did her half sister Emilie's husband, Benjamin Hardin Helm. The Lincolns had become very attached to "Little Sister" Emilie, who loved them in return. The Lincolns also felt close to Emilie's husband Ben, so when word of Ben's death reached them, the family grieved with Emilie, welcoming her into the White House, where Lincoln's friends and foes all objected to harboring an avowed Confederate within the home of the highest leader of the Union.

Though Mary undoubtedly grieved for the loss of family members, she publicly made her position clear. Those members of her family who had chosen to actively support the Confederacy had turned their backs on the nation and on her husband. She declared that she would not grieve for any of them, that they had made their choice. She felt that her brothers and brothers-in-law serving in the Confederate army would have gladly seen her husband defeated or even killed. How could she sympathize with that?

Still, Mary's critics saw her as a Southern sympathizer because of her family ties with the Southern culture in Kentucky, though Kentucky officially stayed with the Union. The state was torn, and many accused Mary of being disloyal or even of being an actual traitor and spy. There was suspicion that members of her family also used the Lincoln connection to benefit the Confederacy. One of Mary's half sisters was accused of using the Lincoln name as a means of smuggling contraband in her trunks, perhaps medicines for wounded soldiers, which were in short supply, and even an elegant new uniform for Confederate president Jefferson Davis.

Another of Mary's family members, David Todd, brought bitter recrimination to the Lincolns when he was accused of mistreating Union prisoners of war at Libby Prison, which he commanded. Prison conditions were already bad enough as the number of captives steadily increased. Starvation, inadequate clothing and bedding, severe overcrowding and terrible outbreaks of contagious diseases that decimated prison populations were common problems. How much worse to see a family member of the president of the United States accused of mistreatment of Union prisoners?

The Todd family was not the only one bringing serious shame and humiliation through split sympathies. The Breckinridge family suffered similar divisions. Reverend Robert Jefferson Breckinridge, a man of strong reputation for the Union, found himself filled with dismay when family members declared for the South and secession. Well educated, of rich family heritage, involved in law, politics and religion, Robert stood among the highest levels of the famous in the state of Kentucky. He had established himself

Reverend Robert J. Breckinridge.
Courtesy of Library of Congress.

as antislavery despite owning slaves. He became an ardent spokesman for gradual emancipation, as well as colonization of slaves.

As a father figure for his nephew John C. Breckinridge, he must have felt great pride in the young man's rapid rise to political power. He watched as John served in various levels of leadership, including as vice president with Buchanan and as candidate for president in the 1860 election (though Lincoln won) and as senator. How much greater must the disappointment have been when his beloved nephew resigned his Senate seat to eventually fight for the Confederacy, becoming a general in the Southern army and, toward the war's end, the secretary of war? That was hard enough for a staunch Unionist and antislavery man.

Worse yet, his own offspring began choosing the other side as well. His son Robert Jr. stood for the South, going off to fight against the Union. Another son, William C.P. Breckinridge, also chose to fight for the Confederacy, as did a son-in-law, Theophilus Steel. On the other hand, his son Joseph fought for the Union army, as did three other sons-in-law. The family had been torn asunder as surely as the nation had. Reverend Breckinridge, though, evidently never wavered in his support of the Union. According to Ranck in the *History of Fayette County*, "In the late war, he took sides with the National Government, and exerted all of his great powers in support of the administration." Furthermore, Ranck wrote, "He was a man of indomitable will and unquestioned courage, and during the great civil conflict, he rose to his greatest height as a writer, statesman and patriot."

Another prominent family that suffered serious division was the household of John J. Crittenden, a major political figure from the state of Kentucky. His accomplishments in national leadership were legion, and he stood firm for the Union. In a last-ditch effort to save the nation from war, Crittenden presented a compromise plan, in the tradition of Henry Clay, who had died in 1852, well before the conflict began. Crittenden's tremendous efforts to prevent the war failed, and when the country toppled into conflict, Crittenden, too, found himself with a divided family. Two of Crittenden's sons who stepped up to serve—one, George Bibb becoming a major general for the Confederacy, and another, Thomas Leonidas, becoming a major general for the Union—were arguably elevated in large part due to their name.

A grandson, John Crittenden Coleman, fought for the Confederacy, dying in 1862. In addition, nephew Thomas Turpin Crittenden was a Union general, and sons Robert and Eugene and another grandson John Crittenden Watson all fought for the Union. Though his family was torn asunder by the great conflict, still Crittenden supported all of his family, doing his best on their behalf.

In the Benjamin Gratz family, the patriarch himself was staunchly pro-Union, a man of prominence in the community, friend of the late Henry Clay and instrumental in creating a monument to honor the statesman. Gratz served as a trustee of Transylvania University most of his life in Lexington, held the position of second president for the Lexington & Ohio Railroad, was known as a prestigious businessman and helped establish both the public library and Orphan Asylum along with his first wife. So enthusiastic was Gratz about preserving the Union that he, according to the *History of Fayette County*, "at various times turned his residence into a commissariat depot and cook-house for companies of Federal soldiers."

When his first wife died, Gratz married Anna, Orville Shelby's widow. Gratz became stepfather to her son, Joseph O. Shelby, and when the Civil War began, Jo Shelby, then living in Missouri, immediately declared himself for the Confederacy, entering into the heat of the fighting. One of Benjamin Gratz's sons from his first marriage, Cary Gist Gratz, joined the Union forces and fought on the same field of battle as Jo Shelby. Captain Cary Gratz died in battle on August 10, 1861, and was the first fallen soldier of the Civil War to be buried at the Lexington Cemetery. His half sister Miriam described his death and funeral in her Civil War journal and made it quite clear that she and her family were firm for the Union.

Though Henry Clay did not live to see the Civil War, which he had worked so tirelessly to prevent, his sons and grandsons chose opposing sides when the war actually broke out. Two of his sons followed their father's example and stayed firm for the Union; one of them, Thomas, kept a line of communication open with President Lincoln, acting as the president's man in Lexington. Thomas also sent the president a keepsake from Lincoln's near-idol Henry Clay, a snuffbox the great orator especially valued. Lincoln wrote back thanking Thomas for the gift and expressing his pleasure at receiving a memento of the man who held the Union together with his Compromise of 1850.

But one of Henry Clay's sons, James Brown Clay, held Southern sympathies, choosing to leave the country and remain in exile in Canada until his death on January 26, 1864, before the war ended. His son James B. Clay Jr. signed up to fight for the Confederacy, serving much of his military career with General John C. Breckinridge, going with Breckinridge when he was called to become secretary of war for the Confederacy toward the war's end.

Three other grandsons of the Great Compromiser fought for the Confederacy as well as James B. Jr., Eugene Erwin, Henry Boyle Clay and Thomas Julian Clay all fought in the CSA army, with Thomas dying in 1863 during the war. Two grandsons of the great orator fought for the Union, Henry Clay McDowell and Henry Clay III, who died in 1862.

What a painful irony when a man like Henry Clay, who lived and breathed devotion to his country and to keeping the Union intact, who vowed that he was a Union man through and through, would have sons and grandsons fighting against the Union he so devotedly gave his strength and health to protect.

Though so many families were torn asunder by the brothers' war, some families like the Morgans stood united in their devotion to one side or the other. For the Morgans, their loyalties lay with the South. Son John Hunt Morgan became a legendary figure among Southerners, striking at the heart of the enemy through those hit-and-run raids of his, as well as the long-distance raid up into Indiana and Ohio, where he spread fear and confusion wherever he went. His brothers at some point all rode with him, and Thomas Morgan lost his life during battle while following John. In addition to his brothers fighting with John, his brother-in-law, Basil Duke, of course fought at his side, second in command through a large portion of the war, assuming command of Morgan's men after Morgan lost his own life. Married to John Morgan's sister Tommie, Duke shared his brother-in-law's devotion to the Southern cause and carried on what he realized was a hopeless struggle after his leader, friend and brother-in-law died.

John Morgan's sister Kitty wed a Confederate supporter, as well, General A.P. Hill, who was killed in the fighting only seven days before Lee

General A.P. Hill. *Courtesy of Library of Congress.*

surrendered at Appomattox Court House. Throughout the war, this family stood united in their service to the Confederacy. But even in such a solid front, slight chinks appeared, as when John's former brother-in-law from his first marriage, Sanders Bruce, who was also his business partner before the war, stood solidly for the Union. Likewise united in loyalty to the North were the Blair men, Francis Preston, Frank Jr. and Montgomery.

So many families split along sectional lines during the conflict between Southern and Northern states. Households broke up, friendships dissolved and neighbors became suspicious of one another throughout Lexington and much of the nation. After the warfare ceased, there were endless divisions and hard feelings that needed mending just as the nation overall needed to mend and heal. For some, the break would never mend. For others, family and bonds of friendship won out over hard feelings and distrust.

Chapter 9

Abraham Lincoln and His Bluegrass Bride

T he day must have looked perfect to them as they enjoyed their carriage ride together. No more anxiety about the future. No more fears or worries. No more nightmarish, bloody war. Mary and her beloved Abraham must have felt they were experiencing the best day of their time as president and first lady of the nation. They relaxed together, talked of their future, what they might do when his second term ended—he favored traveling. They spoke of putting the past behind them and moving ahead into a brighter future. Both knew they must put aside the devastating grief that had plagued their lives—lost children, lost parents, lost friends.

They had so much to celebrate. Richmond had fallen. Lee had surrendered. The Confederacy had shattered. Now would begin the remaking of the nation. Lincoln had to feel a mighty relief. He'd managed, somehow, to hold the Union together, to drag the torn nation through the greatest crisis of its history and give the country a fresh start. What an enormous weight must have lifted from his shoulders. They were scheduled to attend the theater that night, and though neither actually felt like going, they would not disappoint the crowds who would attend that night in hopes of seeing them. The theater had already promoted their promised presence. They couldn't break that promise.

The performance was a comedy, and oh, how Lincoln loved a good comedy, a chance to lean back in the rocking chair especially provided for him in the presidential box, throw back his head full of shaggy hair and laugh

President Abraham Lincoln. *Courtesy of Library of Congress.*

until tears ran down his deeply grooved cheeks. Mary must have delighted in seeing how relaxed he was, how full of hope, how cheered. She snuggled as close as possible, loving to be near him, loving the closeness restored between them now that his preoccupation with war would be gone. They held hands.

Neither noticed the shadowy figure creeping in behind them. Neither was aware of the malicious intent of that man. And neither had any premonition at that moment of the terrible danger stalking them, despite their belief in dreams and supernatural warnings. By the next morning, Mary would be a widow, left to struggle with what remained of her life without the husband she adored, without the future they'd envisioned. Mary's life would, in essence, end at the same moment a bullet pierced her husband's brain. She would never be the same. She would wrestle with mental disintegration and emotional collapse for the rest of her life before finally joining him in death. The wedding ring Abraham gave her had promised "Love is eternal."

They'd been drawn to each other when they first met in Springfield, Illinois, where Mary moved to stay with her older sister for the main purpose of finding a suitable husband. That was the agenda for young women of the day. Marriage was the sole career option for most women. The better the marriage, the further in life a woman could go. For Mary Todd, the sky was the limit. She already knew what her future held. She'd intended from childhood to marry a president. The obvious choice, statesman Henry Clay, the political lion of her home community, Lexington, Kentucky, already had a wife.

Mary's father was a political man, always fascinated by the ins and outs of politics, and Mary grew up passionately interested in the political world of her father. Perhaps, as some suggest, that was her connection with a busy parent who had little time for his large and boisterous family. Mary could talk politics with the best of them. Plus, as she grew, she spent her weeks at an elegant boarding school located near Ashland, the home of her idol, Henry Clay, the man who hoped to be president. Mary was not unique in her expectation that Clay would reach the highest office in the land. Everyone in town believed that. In fact, possibly everyone in the nation believed that, though somehow it never quite happened. He came close but never close enough.

Mary adored Clay and stopped by unannounced for informal visits. Later, when she, her husband and their two young sons spent three weeks in her hometown while Lincoln was on his way to Washington to begin what he expected to be his national political career, Mary must have found a way for those two men she adored to meet. Though there's no genuine documentation to prove that Clay and Lincoln met face to face, it's hard to believe that proud, ambitious Mary would not have arranged for these two men to be introduced. Besides, she well knew that her husband greatly admired the "Sage of Ashland." Mary had never been shy around Clay, barging in on him for visits even when he was busy. There's no reason to think she would have hesitated to bring Lincoln to meet his near-idol, "Harry of the West."

When Mary and Abraham first met in those early days in Springfield, they had some rough spots. Despite a broken engagement and lengthy separation, the two politically minded and ambitious young people got back together, met quietly to reestablish their relationship and then orchestrated a quick marriage in Mary's sister Elizabeth's parlor. Katherine Helm, their niece, would later write, "They were one in mind and heart and as long as life lasted neither ever again doubted the other's faithful love." Though her family had objections to the union, they could not stand against Mary once she gave her heart to her "tall Kentuckian." Mary's family looked askance at Lincoln. They questioned his family background, his lack of education and polish, his accumulated debt and doubtful prospects for the future. Mary's family wasn't so sure about this awkward, lanky country boy.

Mary was sure. She felt drawn to Lincoln from the very first. She had her pick of fine young men with great promise, men like Stephen Douglas and a grandson of Patrick Henry. Mary came from quality, and her family expected her to marry brilliantly. Lincoln did not meet their standards. But he did meet hers. She saw something in him that wasn't always apparent to others. She saw past the rough exterior to the brilliant mind beneath, to the savvy wit and strength of character, not to mention the drive and dedication that brought him from a farm cabin into the drawing rooms of Springfield, from dirt-poor backwoods life to educated society. Mary saw a bright future for the two of them together, and she refused to give up on him.

Their start was as doubtful as her family envisioned. They lived in a boardinghouse among people of far lesser status than Mary was accustomed to. She'd been raised in the heart of the Bluegrass, in a family of wealth and prestige, in a home where no one had to do manual labor, where slaves carried the workload, leaving women free to pursue social niceties. In her new life, the work was up to Mary. That early life had its problems but also its joys. Mary and Abraham labored together to hammer out a career for him in law but also in their beloved politics. They subscribed to newspapers and kept up with all the latest thought. They read together, often with Mary reading aloud for him while he unwound. They began their family; both were deeply loving and highly indulgent parents.

Lincoln's background is, of course, too well known to need detail here, but his youth seemed so totally unlike hers that they must have nothing in common. Yet the two got along famously, sharing a strong sense of humor, that love of their children, their intelligence—Mary was more thoroughly educated than most women of the time—their ambitions and a quiet sadness over the losses in their lives. Both had lost beloved mothers early.

Their lives moved along at an ordinary pace. He practiced law and edged around the center of his true love, politics. She kept the home in elegance and high style as they moved upward, buying their own house and entertaining nicely. She read books for him and summed them up. He trusted her judgement. She made clothes for him and their boys, being sure everyone under her roof dressed well and knew their manners, not always an easy task with a husband who neither knew nor cared about such niceties. She always kept a comb handy to tackle his unruly hair. He steadfastly ignored the worst of her emotional outbursts.

When Lincoln got himself elected to Congress, both he and Mary were delighted. Now they were on track for the real thing. In high excitement, they stopped off on their way to Washington to visit the Todd clan in Lexington. They spent a leisurely three weeks, which many commentators believe gave Lincoln an up-close look at slavery that he might not have seen before. Lincoln wasn't unaware of slavery by any means. He'd seen slavery throughout his lifetime, even staying with a friend in a slave household previously. He'd seen slaves manacled and being shipped to auction. He wasn't ignorant of the peculiar institution, but perhaps he had not previously seen the crueler side as closely as he did now.

Mary's home held a full staff of slaves to meet every household need. Her grandmother's home, which they probably visited, stood near the slave pens, where men, women and children were kept imprisoned until being sold. Lincoln undoubtedly loitered at the courthouse to exchange funny stories with other lawyers, a favorite activity of his. And while there, most likely he witnessed Lexington's notorious slave auctions or even a whipping at the public whipping post. He likely spoke with men in Lexington who owned slaves. Lexington was fast becoming the largest slave auction center in the state. Besides, the Lincolns subscribed to Lexington papers and would have been familiar with ads for slave sales or notices about escaped slaves.

Lincoln knew slavery, and he hated it. He said so himself. He saw himself as always hating slavery. Yet he valued the views of Henry Clay, who spoke out against slaveholding, favoring gradual emancipation and colonization for freed slaves, all while being a slaveholder himself. Lincoln expressed his views in speeches, speaking against the expansion of slavery into the territories. In the earlier portion of his presidency, he advocated keeping hands off the slave states and their way of life. He just wanted to keep slavery from expanding. Clearly his first priority, as was that of his mentor and "beau ideal of a statesman" Henry Clay, was maintaining the Union.

Newly elected, Lincoln was on his way to Washington with the high hopes of himself and his wife. However, Mary and the boys soon headed back to her hometown, while Lincoln immersed himself in national business, though he did not seem to leave his mark behind when he left at term's end. Discouraged at that point in his career, Lincoln seemed ready to retreat, spend his life lawyering and make the best of it. Mary, who always encouraged him and believed in him with a fierce determination, would not see it that way. Even when he yielded to melancholy, Mary never gave up on him.

He felt the stir of political itchiness again and rose up to meet the challenge, facing Senator Stephen Douglas in a series of debates that caught the nation's eye. Seven times they faced off against each other, with Lincoln declaring himself for freedom for all mankind, regardless of race or anything else. Some of Lincoln's most quotable lines stem from those debates. He famously announced, "A house divided against itself cannot stand." He went on to say, "I believe this government can not endure permanently half slave, and half free." The debates drew strong opinions from the state and the nation. Though Douglas won the election and retained his Senate seat, Lincoln, this time, made his mark.

Sinking back into what he expected to be oblivion, Lincoln felt that familiar surge of melancholy rise in him. Mary would have none of it. She refused to let him give up on himself and his future. She did not much care for the offer he received to become a provisional governor off in the middle of nowhere. Mary was surely delighted when her husband won the presidential nomination from his new Republican Party. Hadn't she always believed in him? He faced three opponents: John C. Breckinridge, his old nemesis Stephen Douglas and John Bell. The election was hard fought, and Lincoln forced himself to stay on the sidelines, aware of what a precarious balance hung over the election. He understood that too much emancipationist talk would drive away the South and too much moderation on slavery would alienate the Northern abolitionists.

Lincoln won the presidency of the United States, and immediately the South rustled in restless preparations. The dominoes toppled, and seven states seceded before he was even sworn in March 4. By April, war had fallen upon the nation he loved, and Lincoln devoted himself and every resource at his disposal to holding the Union together. He could not allow the nation to crumble when his idol Henry Clay had sacrificed everything to preserve

Lincoln and son. *Courtesy of Library of Congress*.

it. No man would want to be the first president of the United States to allow sectional divisions to destroy the unity that bound the nation together.

Lincoln, like Jefferson Davis, struggled with problems in waging war, in finding the right men for each job, in pushing his generals to confront former comrades in arms and in reaching a speedy conclusion to the bloody conflict. Nobody expected the war to last as long as it did. Mostly the citizens of both sides expected a quick resolution. The South expected to go its own way, perhaps taking Washington, DC with it. The North expected a quick capitulation and everything back to normal again. Nobody thought both sides would prove so resolute. But when it came to a lengthy war, the North had obvious advantages in manpower over the less-populated South, manufacturing of goods, support from other nations and more access to supplies of all sorts.

Mary was less prepared for war. She'd spent a lifetime dreaming of living in the White House. She expected she and Abraham would lead the social

Mary Todd Lincoln, first lady. *Courtesy of Library of Congress.*

life of the capital, shine among society there and hold dinners and balls to delight the nation, and she would be the perfect hostess. She'd been trained throughout her well-bred youth to excel at the very skills required by the highest position open to a woman in the land. She knew how to dress well, how to entertain, how to redecorate a house falling into ruin, how to shop for the finest, how to speak French and dance the latest dances. Throughout their marriage, she and Abraham worked together to reach their dream. Mary was perfectly suited to be first lady.

She was not, however, perfectly suited for war, death and destruction. She was not suited for grief. Loss left her emotionally shattered. She had already lost her mother when young, her father and grandmother within months of one another and her little boy Eddie while they lived in Springfield, and now she would lose her beloved son Willie while in the White House. Each loss left her less able to cope with the next. When the half sister she and Lincoln loved best lost her Confederate officer husband on the battlefield, both Lincoln and Mary grieved with her. They welcomed "Little Sister"

Emilie into the White House, where critics whispered and even spoke aloud against such treasonous wartime behavior.

Mary's Southern family counted against her, and critics called her a traitor and a spy for the Confederacy. Her skills as hostess and redecorator of the president's home got her into even more trouble. She was called extravagant and wasteful during wartime. Her choice of elaborate wardrobe got her in equal difficulty with her enemies, who seemed to be everywhere. And under pressure, her weaknesses got worse, not better. Shopping soothed her wounded spirit, until the bills came due, while she tried to hide her debts from her husband and numerous critics.

On top of everything else, her husband kept so busy dealing with war plans and tactics that she hardly spent any time with him. Their close partnership faded, and Mary felt shut out, lonely and overwhelmed. She trusted her dressmaker with her fears and troubles. Elizabeth Keckley, a freedwoman, quickly became more than a dressmaker for Mary. She became a friend and confidante, closer than a sister, always there for Mary and her family. It would be Lizzie that Mary called for when the president was shot and dying. It would be Lizzie who stood by her when her world crumbled. But it would also be Lizzie who wrote a tell-all book about the inside world of the Lincoln family, and Mary would never trust her former confidante again.

The war dragged on and on. Mary's older son signed up, despite her panicky fears. Her husband ignored death threats and plots against him. Mary took them to heart and feared for his safety. The war could not end soon enough for Mary. But meanwhile, there was the next election to deal with and all her fears and secrets to be kept from her war-weary husband. Though he did not feel at all certain of reelection, Lincoln won a second term, and he gave the speech of a lifetime for his second inaugural address, while in the crowd a famous actor stood watching. Close study of a photo of the scene reveals John Wilkes Booth, who would shoot and kill Lincoln a few days later, right there in the watching crowd. Lincoln spoke of hope and unity. He would not be a man of vengeance once the fighting ended. He would bring peace for the nation's future.

Indisputably, Lincoln's greatest achievement beyond holding together the Union would be the Emancipation Proclamation that first freed only the slaves in rebellious states. Freed slaves were urged to join the military to fight for the Union. Eventually, all slaves would be freed, so that the peculiar

Second Inauguration. Published in *Harper's Weekly*, March 18, 1865. *Courtesy of Douglas W. Bostick.*

institution in the South and throughout the entire nation would cease to exist and the adjustment to a new way of life would begin.

Then came the end. Richmond fell. Lee surrendered. The Confederacy collapsed, and the North celebrated. Banners and gunfire expressed the joy and hope for the nation. And the Lincolns were looking ahead to a future that would not come as they entered the theater where their life together would end.

Chapter 10

Jefferson Davis at Transylvania

In the garden together with his wife, Varina, Jefferson Davis quietly worked at cutting rose clippings. This peaceful, homey scene, hinting at a shared warmth and closeness as husband and wife tended their garden, would not last. Davis had resigned his seat in the United States Senate, unable to stay in that position now that his home state, Mississippi, had seceded from the Union. Politics had been a central part of his life for years now, but perhaps he would leave politics behind. Perhaps he would spend more time at home with his family, tend to the needs of the plantation and lead a quieter life.

That was not to be, however. A messenger arrived to interrupt the contentment of the day. When Jefferson Davis read the message, his wife watched his face. Later, in her memoirs about her husband, she described his reaction: "When reading the telegram he looked so grieved that I feared some evil had befallen our family." She went on to explain, "After a few minutes of painful silence he told me, as a man might speak of a sentence of death." Jefferson Davis had just received word that he'd been chosen as president of the newly formed Confederate States of America.

This was not good news, nor was it anything that Davis would have chosen if given a choice. In fact, according to Varina, he said:

> As this had been suggested as a probable event, and what appeared to me adequate precautions had been taken to prevent it, I was surprised, and still more, disappointed...I had not believed myself as well suited to the office as some others. I thought myself better adapted to command in the field, and

Jefferson Davis. *Courtesy of Library of Congress.*

Mississippi had given me the position which I preferred to any other—the highest rank in her army.

Davis saw himself as a fighting man, then, a leader in military matters, a man better suited for battle plans than for diplomacy and headship of the newly formed Southern nation.

Davis expected this call to the presidency of the Confederacy to be a brief period, a time of transition until someone better suited to the job could be chosen. However, Jefferson Davis would be the one and only president of the Confederate States of America. He would lead this brand-new nation in war. He would struggle to hammer out the origins of this new nation, and he would stand ready to defend the CSA with every ounce of his resolve. He gave himself body, mind and spirit to the South and served his new nation the best he knew how. That the nation perished was laid at his feet. The blame for that failure fell on his shoulders, yet there are some who say the task was doomed from the beginning, that no one else could have done any better than did Jefferson Davis.

He began life in what is now Fairview, Kentucky, in current Todd County, roughly one hundred miles from the birthplace of another Kentuckian who would find himself leading a nation at war, Abraham Lincoln. Both men were tall for their time. Both men developed a great love of reading, and both found themselves forced to make hard decisions and served as leaders in the face of great challenges and difficulties. Both lived in White Houses barely one hundred miles apart, Lincoln's in Washington, D.C., and Davis's in Richmond, Virginia. And both were roughly the same age, less than a year apart.

Davis grew up surrounded by comfort and wealth, accustomed to slave workers, part of a large family, the last of ten children. The family moved and settled in Mississippi, so Davis grew up with strong Southern ties and a sense of the agrarian culture of the South. Because his family treated slaves with consideration and dignity, providing privileges that were not widespread among slaveholding families, Davis never could accept the assertions about harshness and cruelties in slave life. His view of slavery seems almost idealized, though he had to have seen some of the harshness and degradation of slavery.

Growing up in a fine family, Jefferson Davis found himself enrolled at Transylvania University in Lexington, Kentucky. That was the place for young men of good families to go. He associated with youth who went on to positions of leadership throughout the nation. Transylvania, the oldest institution of higher education west of the Allegheny Mountains, provided a prestigious environment, a classical education, social skills, an extensive library, distinguished faculty and exposure to diplomatic training not available elsewhere in the South or the West. Transylvania produced a bumper crop of governors, senators, congressmen, generals, doctors, lawyers and judges.

Contacts made at the worthy institution would stand Davis in good stead for the remainder of his life. He made lifelong friends there, developed skills as an orator and debater, honed his abilities through dedicated study and became a man of honor and dignity. Some debate exists about how long

Davis stayed at the university, since records are not always available. Several seriously damaging fires destroyed some records, plus the university devolved until it almost ceased existence entirely through a series of unfortunate events, though later Transylvania would return to prominence.

Davis himself said he spent three years at Transylvania, three years during which he succeeded, made his mark on campus and city, achieved much and felt good about his accomplishments. He was chosen to present an oration on friendship and did the job well. During his time at the university, he boarded with one of the city's most distinguished leaders, newspaper editor and postmaster Joseph Ficklin, who became a lifelong friend. Varina noted that on a visit to the city her husband daily stopped by to see his old friend. The Ficklin household attracted not only several students to board there but also notable individuals of the day who enjoyed discussion and debate among themselves. Davis would have been exposed to a wide range of political ideas and current thought.

A classmate of Davis described him, as quoted by Varina, as being "the first scholar, ahead of all his classes, and the bravest and handsomest of all the college boys." Davis was said to have scholarly habits yet enjoyed fun as well as anyone else. He never cared much for sports, read frequently, never indulged in anything the least bit immoral and seemed overall to be a gentleman of high standards and conscience. Davis was popular, admired by his classmates and known to be a kind person. His friends included a son of famed statesman Henry Clay; Davis and Henry Clay Jr. would be close after their time at Transylvania, and Davis would visit the Clay home, Ashland, numerous times. Furthermore, by the time Davis reached the United States Senate, he had encountered a half dozen or more Transylvania classmates who also served as senators from their home states.

Davis's time at Transylvania was not yet over when he got word of his father's death, which hit him hard. His older brother Joseph stepped into the gap to act as a surrogate father for young Jefferson. Joseph pulled some strings and got his brother a place at West Point Military Academy. Jefferson Davis would not have chosen to leave Transylvania and Lexington early. He did not look forward to moving from being top of his class, star student and valued scholar to starting from scratch at West Point. But he did his duty, a trait that would stay with him the rest of his life. He did what needed to be done, whether it was his first choice or not. He did the right thing by his brother.

So, reluctantly but obediently, Jefferson Davis moved on to the military academy, where he did not excel. He received demerits on a couple of occasions and almost got thrown out. He apparently missed his friends and the congenial environment at Transylvania. Davis spent the next four years at West Point. He did what he needed to do, though not with great enthusiasm evidently. He did not finish high in his class, but he finished. While there, according to Varina, Davis rescued classmates from a fire and also saved a building from great damage. He sent money home to his mother, suffered an injury that kept him out of action for some time and again made friendships and contacts that lasted him all his life. Many of the men he trusted with leadership during the Civil War had been his companions during his West Point years.

Once finished at West Point, Davis embarked on a military career that took him, according to one story, back to Lexington while recruiting for the military. While he was there, a cholera outbreak occurred, according to some sources who say that Davis ceased his recruiting efforts to help with the epidemic. He went on to fight in the war against Mexico, where his good friend from Transylvania and West Point, Henry Clay Jr., was wounded and died. Davis returned from the fighting as a hero, a respected and popular war veteran who then continued his lifelong interest in politics.

His first marriage to Colonel Zachary Taylor's daughter Sarah Knox ended with her death of malaria shortly after they wed. He later wed Varina Howell, who stood by him through trials and troubles before, during and after the war. Through Varina's writing efforts a record of Davis's life remains, which opens a window into his thoughts and feelings, as well as her own.

Davis got heavily involved with politics, serving in several roles, including as secretary of war under President Franklin Pierce, a task he took to heart and did extremely well. He strengthened the United States military, improving conditions and providing better weaponry and tactics, which takes on a heavy sense of irony since this is the very military Davis would face when he accepted leadership of the new nation and began establishing a Southern military force. Davis was then elected as a senator from Mississippi, and in that role, he revealed strong feelings about states' rights. He acquired a reputation on the Senate floor as a spokesman for the South and a believer in the right to secede, at least theoretically. While he believed in states' rights, Jefferson Davis did not want to see the nation divided. He did not want to see states seceding even if he believed they had the right, and he did not want to see his nation at war with itself.

Nevertheless, states seceded, including his own, and Davis was forced to bid farewell to the Senate, a task that took a great toll on his strength and health. Sick for a week, he yet managed to stand before his fellow senators and a huge crowd of onlookers. Varina wrote that she wondered if the "festive crowd" could see what she saw, "his deep depression, his desire for reconciliation, and his overweening love for the Union in whose cause he had bled, and to maintain which he was ready to sacrifice all but liberty and equality." She described his speech: "Unshed tears were in it, and a plea for peace permeated every tone...He was listened to in profound silence, broken only by respected applause."

Varina noted, "Not his wife alone, but all who sat spellbound before him knew how genuine was his grief, and entered into the spirit of his loving appeal...There was scarcely a dry eye in the multitude as he took his seat with the words, 'It only remains for me to bid you a final adieu.'" Varina could see what it cost her husband to resign his Senate seat, to give up on unity for his nation, to walk away from the service he loved and the men he admired and respected and who felt the same for him. It was not an easy decision, and it was not something he did eagerly. Jefferson Davis did not want to see his country split apart, nor did he want to serve as president of the new nation. He did what was required of him, and he did it to the very best of his ability.

Beginning a new nation demanded great effort and large amounts of diplomacy. Jefferson Davis needed to forge together states that had just asserted their right to independence and freedom. Binding these individual states into a working, unified nation would require every ounce of statesmanship he could scrape together. Then there was the looming war to handle. The tasks before him would have been daunting for anyone. His single-minded determination to get that nation formed and hold it together marked the key to his presidency. Perhaps his greatest weakness in the position was his certainty that everyone else involved would dedicate themselves as totally to the tasks at hand.

Davis juggled jobs seemingly tirelessly as he formed a government and braced his new nation for war. However, his health had long since been seriously undermined by injuries and lingering results from malaria.

Throughout his presidency, there would be weeks when he conducted business from his sickbed, and there would be rumors that he lay on his deathbed. Not everyone felt sympathy for his bouts of illness. For starters, his generals bickered among themselves and at times outright defied his orders. Davis, as a hands-on manager, kept tight control of just about every aspect of his government. As some historians point out, Davis acted like his own secretary of war, which made a lot of sense since he'd excelled at the job when he held it himself previously for the United States.

His critics felt he was too hands-on, squandering his time and often-limited energies on tasks of lesser importance. Some also felt that he depended too heavily on men from his past, trusting generals who did not always live up to his expectations. Further, critics suggest that Davis did not select his generals and other men in high office with much insight or discernment, plus he was then loyal to a fault. Whatever the case, this was a man struggling to raise an army from a reluctant population who at times paid for a substitute instead of serving themselves.

The South had resources far more limited than those of the North: a shortage of manufacturing, a shortage of manpower and a shortage of funding. Though Davis tried, he could not win recognition for his fledgling nation from potential allies overseas. On the battlefield, generals with conflicting agendas did not always coordinate their attacks or press their advantage. And at times, when Davis called for more men, the state governors essentially let him know they'd think about it.

So perhaps, as some historians point out, the South was doomed from the start, especially when the war dragged on far longer than anyone seemed to expect. Perhaps the South underestimated the determination shown by President Lincoln to hold the Union together whatever it took. Perhaps the South expected a quick, decisive victory that would crush the Federal enthusiasm for war. Or perhaps the South simply expected to walk away with no hard feelings.

And as the Confederacy crumbled, Davis refused to admit that defeat stared him in the face. When Lee faltered and failed, Davis kept on hoping somehow Lee would pull off a miracle. When Davis got word that he would have to evacuate Richmond, he hesitated as long as possible, hoping for some last-minute reprieve. When he finally left the Confederate capital, the North celebrated the victory, assuming that the war had ended with Lee's surrender and the fall of Richmond. Jefferson Davis simply saw both as setbacks. He did not accept that the war was over.

Surrounded by cabinet members and military leaders who knew the war was done for the Confederacy, still Davis persisted. He wanted to keep fighting. He wanted to head deeper south and join up with generals who had not surrendered. He wanted to press on, somehow. The men around him were forced to make it clear to their president. The war had ended. The Confederacy had collapsed. There was no more country for him to lead.

His secretary of war at the end, John C. Breckinridge, former United States vice president, urged Davis to escape and made arrangements to protect the president of the fallen nation. Basil Duke helped divert the enemy to protect the president and aid in his escape. Davis fled but did so far too slowly to suit the men who implored him to make good his escape. Those men understood the terrible danger. By this time, they all knew President Abraham Lincoln had been killed. They all knew the Federal government put a price on their heads, accusing them of complicity in Lincoln's death. They all knew that the primary target of Union vengeance would be Jefferson Davis.

Nothing got him moving any faster, and some feared he simply did not intend to escape. The others made a run for it, some more successfully than others. Davis lingered until Federal troops showed up to surround him and his family. He was captured, accused of treason, arrested and imprisoned. At last he was forced to accept that the South was done. His new nation had crumbled into dust. He would face the next long months in a prison cell, with his health failing and his fate uncertain. Even so, he remained undaunted. He did not confess to any wrongdoing. He did not ask for pardon, and he did not beg for mercy.

Since the United States had no idea what to do with him, his imprisonment dragged on. Friends petitioned for his release. The government did not want to make a martyr of him. Nor did it have a strong case against him for anything. Though he was considered a possible conspirator in the death of Lincoln, nothing existed to tie him to the crime. He could not actually be charged with treason for a number of reasons, including the Federal government's own recognition of the Confederacy as a separate nation with prisoner of war exchanges. Eventually, he was released on bail, pardoned when the general amnesty passed and was free to leave the country for a time.

Jefferson Davis in prison. *Courtesy of Library of Congress.*

He and his family would end up back in the South, where he tried various avenues in business before settling down to write his memoirs, enjoy his grandchildren, speak at Confederate reunions and nurse his ill health, which at last brought his life to an end on December 6, 1889. The living embodiment of a defeated nation, Jefferson Davis would forever represent the "Lost Cause."

Chapter 11

Medical Men

D r. Robert Peter wasn't born an American. He hailed from Cornwall, England, and moved to the United States with his parents when he was a child. Living in several different states with his parents, Peter became a naturalized citizen and then settled in Lexington, Kentucky, married and started a large family. When the Civil War began, no native-born American could have been as solidly pro-Union as Dr. Peter. He stood firm for the unity of the nation, instilling that same patriotic fervor in his family, including teenage Frances, whose war diary opens up an intimate view of the city during the war years. So firmly did Peter support the Union cause that he steadfastly supported his country while being arrested on three separate occasions during the Confederate military occupation of Lexington.

His daughter Frances chronicled her father's war efforts as senior surgeon of the United States military hospitals in Lexington. Frances had access to hospital internal information through her father's position, and she revealed extensive knowledge in her war journal about the number of wounded at various Lexington hospital locations, as well as details about illness and troop movements as patients came and went after major engagements. Dr. Peter held a serious and responsible position, and young Frances had a close connection with what was going on behind the scenes through her father. In a letter to a family member now held in the University of Kentucky Special Collections, Frances wrote of her father, "Pa…is almost run off his feet and has seven clerks writing all the time."

Dr. Robert Peter. *Courtesy of Robert Peter Manuscript Collection, Transylvania University.*

Even the war diary itself reveals her connection with the hospitals and her father's position. Most of the diaries are composed of hospital order forms stitched together; Frances wrote in small, tight script on the backs of those order forms, managing to cram in plenty of information on what paper she could find access to during war shortages. Also in the family papers at the University of Kentucky, in a transcription of part of Frances Peter's war diary, a relative noted, too, that Robert Peter was a "strong Northern sympathizer" and that he was made "Senior Surgeon in charge of all the hospitals in Lexington." Dr. Peter held a prominent and prestigious role during the war, using his medical training and skills to supervise care for wounded soldiers and those stricken with any of the numerous diseases that plagued the population.

The Peter family lived close to Transylvania's facilities, in an elegant red brick house, still standing to this day. Thus, Dr. Peter, whose life focused for many years in some way on Transylvania, was handy living in sight of the buildings where he studied, received a medical degree, taught, served as medical department librarian and had a range of other duties. Once the war erupted, many Lexington buildings were put to use as medical centers, including whatever buildings remained of Transylvania's formerly impressive educational structures.

Through two of his daughters, Frances and Johanna, Dr. Peter's war efforts, as well as his life after the war, have been closely chronicled, with Frances revealing plenty of details about the hospitalized soldiers and Johanna later completing her father's writing work to produce a history of Transylvania's rise and fall, as well as the collapse of Transylvania's Medical Department.

In April 1862, Frances noted, "There are 300 sick at hospital here." She went on to add a few days later, "300 more soldiers expected at the hospital." In May of the same year, Frances pointed out, "The college has been taken for a hospital & Pa has moved his men from the Short Street hospital up there." Later, she observed that the hospital was preparing for one thousand more, which indicated trouble ahead. It's Frances who recorded her father's difficulties during the Confederate occupation when she wrote, "Pa has been arrested three times." Her father would not swear allegiance to the Southern cause; none of the family would.

Once the Confederate military retreated, giving up their occupancy of Lexington, Frances noted, "Pa resumed command at Hospital No 1." Her war diaries indicated that a number of buildings around the city were pressed into service as hospitals and some as prisons for war prisoners. She tracked illnesses that hit the troops or the city in general, such as an outbreak of diphtheria that caused widespread suffering and death. She reflected the citizens' anxiety about troops living outside in tents when the weather became bitterly cold, and Frances, like many sympathetic Union supporters, worried about the men's health during difficult weather conditions.

It's Frances who noted that in April 1863 her father received orders to break up hospital facilities and send the sick to Cincinnati, where perhaps there may have been less risk of intruding Confederate raids or resident spies. Later, she wrote of smallpox among the troops, which undoubtedly kept her father busy dealing with suffering soldiers. Then, in May 1863, Frances described a devastating fire that left the Medical Hall, used as a hospital, as "blackened ruins." She wrote that the sick were gotten out safely and troops fought the fire. Unfortunately, when Frances died before the end of the war, her insights and observations about the war and her father's role in Lexington medical facilities ended as well.

Her sister Johanna picked up the account of their father's life after the war, his return to a normal life, spending his time with his love of chemistry and research rather than serving as a medical doctor. Johanna took her father's incomplete writing project to trace the history of the then defunct Medical Department and the history of Transylvania itself, and she prepared the material for publication after his death, so that his keen intellect and sharp insights live on through her efforts.

The joint venture begun by Dr. Peter and completed by his daughter Johanna tracked the contributions of Transylvania's Medical Department, showing skilled practitioners, how they served their communities and how many of the most talented medical men transmitted their learning through the institution. In *The History of the Medical Department*, Dr. Peter listed several doctors with a Transylvania connection who served during the Civil War. Samuel Annan, MD, who had served on the faculty at Transylvania in a couple of capacities, became a surgeon for the Confederate States of America during the conflict. A Transylvania medical graduate, Samuel M. Letcher, MD, who also taught at Transylvania, was in charge of a United States General Hospital during the Civil War, though he died in February 1863.

Another Transylvania graduate, Ethelbert Ludlow Dudley, MD, started the *Transylvania Medical Journal* and took an active position during the war. He commanded home guards, served as a colonel with a volunteer regiment and acted as surgeon and physician to the men who served with him. He died of typhoid fever in 1862 and was buried in Lexington. Henry Martyn Skillman, MD, studied medicine and surgery at Transylvania and then went on to teach there as well. During the war, he served as a contract surgeon for the Federal government. Lunsford Pitts Yandell Sr., MD, also taught at Transylvania Medical Department and later served in a hospital during the war.

Transylvania's physicians faced the same hardships the troops faced. Surgeons in the field worked under terrible conditions, racing to save lives. Doctors faced almost impossible odds as they tried to save lives, heal injuries, make quick and difficult decisions about which men could be helped and which could not and do their best to prevent the spread of devastating diseases under dreadful living conditions during a bloody and terrible war.

With few medical supplies and little in the way of assistance, they did their very best with the knowledge and understanding they then possessed.

Diseases that struck towns and communities during this time hit even harder among the crowded army camps, where men drank contaminated water, ate spoiled food when they could get any food at all, slept in tents on sodden ground and pushed themselves beyond endurance. Disease impacted the young men out there fighting more than did the direct effects of the warfare, and the toll was far worse in overcrowded prisons of the time.

Even the finest that Transylvania had trained could not always stem the tide of death and misery that flooded through battlefields and prison camps. But without the training Transylvania had provided in its finest years, how much worse might the death toll have been, how much less the skill to fight against disease and injury? Transylvania, one of the greatest institutions in the nation, and certainly an outstanding institution in the southern and western portions of the nation, produced many of the men who would pit themselves against the ravages of war.

Then there was the interesting and unusual situation for another doctor trained through Transylvania. Luke Pryor Blackburn studied medicine, got a degree from Transylvania in 1835 and devoted his medical skills early on to the fight against some of the most devastating diseases of his time. They struck without warning, causing fear, death and devastation among every age, every income and every status in the nation. Lexington itself suffered several notable epidemics, including destructive cholera outbreaks in 1833 and 1849. Luke Blackburn squared off against more than his share of disease, pitting his skills against the ravages of yellow fever in particular.

In fact, Dr. Blackburn acquired so much experience in the fight against yellow fever that he was considered among the top experts of his day. He instituted quarantines to slow down the spread of the disease, and he also warned against stagnant water, though medical knowledge at the time had no awareness of the link between stagnant water and mosquito breeding or the next link between mosquito bites and spread of the illness.

Blackburn, as well as other established medical practitioners, believed yellow fever could be transmitted from dying patients to healthy individuals through contaminated bedding. So, according to historians, when Dr. Blackburn allegedly decided to institute a program of what would now be called biological warfare toward the latter part of the Civil War, he reportedly began by gathering clothing and linens from dead yellow fever victims. By the best medical understanding of the time, those items would spread disease and death wherever they went. A man who claimed Blackburn had hired him testified to the details of the apparent scheme.

According to Godfrey Hyams, Blackburn volunteered to assist patients during a severe yellow fever epidemic. Hyams insisted that Blackburn quietly acquired contaminated clothes and bedding, packed the items in trunks and shipped them for his alleged accomplice to handle the next step. Blackburn was accused of trying to use contagion against Northern cities with the apparent purpose of weakening the Union from within, spreading panic and death among the civilian populations and undermining the Federal war effort. He even swore that Blackburn hired him to deliver a valise of elegant shirts, also supposedly contaminated with yellow fever, to the White House as a gift for president Abraham Lincoln. Hyams denied carrying out that last assignment. He did, however, take trunks of contaminated clothing to be sold among the ordinary citizens of northern cities, like Washington, D.C., and Norfolk.

The plan failed, but only because yellow fever is not spread by contaminated linens and garments. Yellow fever is spread particularly in hot, steamy, swampy climates where mosquitoes breed and thrive, bite disease victims and then carry the disease to healthy individuals they bite later, transmitting disease and death.

Blackburn never faced trial in the United States. He was never found guilty of the actions attributed to him. He'd established himself in Canada to some extent, and after the war, he returned to Kentucky, where he continued battling the assault of deadly diseases. When a Kentucky community found itself hard hit by yellow fever, Dr. Blackburn devoted his skills and energies to saving lives and became known as the "hero of Hickman." Elected governor of Kentucky shortly after (1879–83), Blackburn became an advocate for prison reform and was called "the father of prison reforms in Kentucky." The accusations about his alleged wartime activities arose during his political campaign, but nothing more came of the whole thing, and Blackburn went on to live a life of purpose and dedication to service in the state of Kentucky.

Though Luke Pryor Blackburn's medical service during the war, if the accused actions actually took place, seemed to clearly violate his oath as a physician, his life taken as a whole revealed a man who sought to preserve lives, to battle against the destructive forces of disease and to serve humankind in any way he possibly could. So many men and women faced difficult choices, terrible circumstances and animosities during the Civil War that might never have affected them otherwise.

Transylvania's medical men stood firm for what they believed and served to the best of their ability, some for the North and some for the South. Their time at Transylvania prepared them to dedicate themselves to using their skills and training to make a difference in the world around them. Their lives were changed by their time in Lexington, and they in turn changed lives by their skills and abilities during the war and beyond.

Chapter 12

Horses for Battle

Joseph Bryan faced serious repercussions for choosing the South. Union forces were on their way to arrest him on a charge of treason. He had "aided the enemy" by providing horses for Confederate forces, and when he provided horses, they were the very best. Bryan's Waveland horses were known far and wide. The man definitely knew horseflesh, and all of Lexington recognized his knowledgeable status. So not only had he provided horses for the enemy, but he'd provided the best. And that was at a time when the North desperately needed good horses.

Throughout the war, cavalries kept up a constant demand for reliable horses. A horse that shied from battle or faltered in a tight spot could cost a man his life. By providing those horses to the South, Bryan had heaped insult on top of injury, and the Union forces were heading in his direction to make him pay for siding with the Confederacy. Bryan had no choice. If he didn't flee the Bluegrass, he faced imprisonment or possibly worse.

So, leaving his beloved Waveland plantation, Joseph Bryan Sr. made his way to the far north to find sanctuary in Canada, being neither the first nor the last Southern sympathizer to flee to the neighbor nation. At times, portions of Canada resembled a Southern colony, packed with men, women and children seeking asylum there.

He must have hated to leave his gorgeous and prosperous plantation, but he had no choice. Bryan came from a truly noble family; his ancestor Sir Francis Bryan had served King Henry VIII in England. And he was a grand-nephew of the famed Kentucky pioneer Daniel Boone. In a community of fine families, Bryan could claim one of the finest. Now he must leave it all behind him, with no guarantee that his home would remain standing until his return. Much of his life thus far he'd been a successful farmer, raising cattle, swine and sheep in addition to his blooded horses. His cash crop was hemp, as with many of the Bluegrass farms. His plantation sprawled across an expanse of rich Bluegrass and had long attracted admirers of fine horses, such as Henry Clay. And as with Henry Clay, Bryan's progeny would eventually lose his treasured home.

When Joseph's son was conscripted to fight for the Union, he paid his way out of the call to arms, as was typical for wealthy, landed young men. The going price to hire a substitute to fight in his place was $300, and he gladly paid the price. According to Ron Bryant, head of the Waveland Museum and a descendant of the family himself, Joseph Henry never worked a day in his life. Joseph Sr. had fled to Canada and then slipped back into Missouri to wait out part of the war with family there. He had been a hard and diligent worker, amassing a fortune, which, as Bryant explains, the son Joseph Henry squandered in short order. Unfortunately, Joseph Henry loved gambling more than was healthy for his means, and after the war he was forced to sell the estate he'd inherited from his prosperous father.

Joseph Sr. had known how important horses would be to the war effort. Without horses, battle plans faltered and failed. Especially in Kentucky, the men who volunteered expected to ride. Kentucky boys were not interested in signing up to walk. They would ride or not go at all. So signing up volunteers from the Bluegrass State depended on allowing them to bring their own horses and join the cavalry units, especially the prestigious Morgan's Raiders. Oh, and most every Kentuckian expected to join up as a captain. It took a bit of persuading to get them to sign up when they couldn't be in charge.

Basil Duke, Morgan's second in command, wrote often in his *Reminiscences* and in his *History of Morgan's Men* about horses and their importance to the troops. Duke understood the value of a good horse. Many a fighting man experienced the distress of having his horse shot out from under him. Some even lost a good many horses that way. Jo Shelby had three or four horses shot from under him in just a single battle. At that rate, a cavalry unit required plenty of replacement horses.

Bluegrass Breeding Ground of Power

Morgan's Raiders always needed good horses. Published in *Harper's Weekly*, August 15, 1863. *Courtesy of Douglas W. Bostick.*

A favorite Kentucky technique for replacing horses was the swap. When Kentucky boys discovered that their mounts were worn out, needed a good long rest and must be replaced, they headed home to the Bluegrass. They might get a furlough to go get themselves some fresh horses. The technique involved finding a field with some fine horses grazing and roaming about by themselves with nobody handy to see what was going on. Then the tired horses would be settled to grazing and roaming the fields while the fresh horses were taken in exchange for the exhausted ones.

Not everybody appreciated having his or her horses swapped, though. Often an owner would show up and protest. Whenever rumor warned that Morgan's men might be in the neighborhood, horse owners hid their horses for safekeeping. When Morgan headed north into Indiana and Ohio, farmers had heard about the Kentuckian's habit of helping himself to horses wherever he found them. Farmers found hollows or woodlands where they could stash their horses until Morgan had gone on past.

When the need for horses got even greater toward the later days of the war, instead of swapping, soldiers simply helped themselves to horses wherever they found them. They called it "pressing" horses into service. Their enemies called it stealing, which was why John Hunt Morgan got the nickname among northerners as being the "King of Horse Thieves." Everybody knew John Morgan recognized a good horse when he came across one.

Basil Duke wrote about the wonderful horses Morgan had ridden, especially his best-loved horse, Black Bess, who was lost when they were forced to leave her behind while ferrying across a river. Duke described Black Bess in poetic terms, writing, "She was the most perfect beauty I have ever beheld—even in Kentucky." And that was saying something. Kentucky horses were known as the finest and best, especially if the rider was a Kentuckian. Duke went on to heap descriptive praises on Bess, explaining that she had both "speed and power," that her tendons were "like steel wires" and that she was a creature of "speed, game, intelligence and grace."

Her loss was a great grief to Morgan, and Duke indignantly noted that a Yankee paraded Bess around the country showing her for a quarter a pop. As Duke put it, "Poor Bess—her spirit must have been broken, or she would have kicked the brute's brains out." Even Kentucky horses were expected to fight Union troops.

Life was not easy for those horses. Cavalry rode hard and fast, particularly Morgan's cavalry. Supplies were often unavailable, especially later in the warfare. The men took the best care of their horses that they possibly could, often making sure their horses were fed and bedded down before they tended to their own needs. But when food ran out, it plain ran out. Many a horse was simply ridden to death, collapsing in exhaustion. Others starved and dropped, unable to go on. And, of course, countless horses died on the battlefield. Horses, clearly, made a larger target than did men. What better way to disable a man than to shoot his horse out from under him?

When the men stopped to rest while on their long raids, they often tethered their horses by their sides, where the horses would graze and stand guard at the same time. The men cared for their horses, partly because a horse could make the difference between life and death and partly because their horses were a central part of their emotional lives. Men cared about their mounts to the point where soldiers were known to weep over fallen horses.

Men from Kentucky especially felt a connection to their horses. Many had grown up riding. They felt as comfortable on a horse as anywhere else. Most would rather ride than walk, of course, and horses were a central part of daily life in Civil War–era Kentucky. When the number of horses ran short, even with the best of horse swaps and pressing, the men had a seemingly unique technique for being sure everybody got to ride. They set up a ride-and-tie plan. Half of the men would mount up and set out first, while the other half began walking. The riders would reach a certain distance, stop, tie their horses and continue on foot. The walkers would catch up to the horses, untie them and set out to ride. This would continue for some time, so that nobody had to walk the whole time. The horses even got to rest some while the walkers caught up to where the animals were tethered.

Many a man during the Civil War developed a strong relationship with a favorite horse, as with John Hunt Morgan and his Black Bess, which Duke described: "Her hide was glossy black, without a hair of white." A steady, patient horse, Black Bess might have lost plenty of those glossy black hairs as Morgan's fans swarmed him and his horse, searching for souvenirs of the South's hero. Clipping with scissors, women in particular carried off a good bit of Morgan's horse's mane and tail. Poor Bess. Then there was General Grant, who rode for a time a horse captured from the plantation owned by Jefferson Davis's brother Joseph. The horse's name? It was called Jeff Davis. So, the Union's premier general rode a horse that shared its name with the president of the Confederacy.

After one terrible battle, Duke described a road so clogged with dead horses that the men could scarcely pick their way through. He counted one hundred fallen and frozen horses, which had most likely been weakened by hunger and exhaustion before their deaths. Duke, as with many Kentucky fighting men, almost seemed more unsettled by the horses' deaths than by the deaths of so many men fallen on the battlefield. Men like Duke, Morgan and so many more understood the nature of their horses and appreciated them, trusted them with their lives and cared for them as they would for a beloved family member.

So many horses were lost through bloody battles, starvation and exhaustion that the entire South suffered. Farmers could not plant their fields without sturdy horses to help with the work. Food grew in shorter and shorter supply. At times, there were no horses to pull the artillery needed for battle, so men took the places of those missing horses. At another time, Duke's men requisitioned teams of mules to ride. This was not what they would otherwise choose, but they took what they could find in desperate times.

The Civil War took a tremendous toll of human lives. Nobody can dispute that fact. Disease and hunger increased that toll. But the nation, especially the South, would suffer an additional great loss with the death of so many valuable horses. What's a cavalry without horses? An infantry unit, that's what. And Kentucky boys, born to ride, brought up in an environment where horses and riding held central position for them, mourned each and every loss. As Colonel Robert W. Black put it in his *Cavalry Raids of the Civil War* about the South, "The entire population was used to horses and all were good riders." Nowhere was this truer than in Kentucky, in the heart of the Bluegrass, Lexington.

Chapter 13
Windows on the War

Whatever motivated Frances Dallam Peter to begin her Civil War journal, nobody in the city of Lexington had a better location for the task. In the family's two-story brick house on a corner by Gratz Park, Frances, or Frank, as her family called her, had a perfect view of Hopemont, the home of John Hunt Morgan's mother, Henrietta, who was notorious for her Southern sympathies. Frances could also see the Gratz home where family friend Miriam lived as near neighbor to the Morgans, too. Transylvania's buildings were within sight and would function as hospital and sometime prison.

When Union forces occupied Lexington, Frances could watch from her window as soldiers pitched tents in Gratz Park. She could count how many men came and went. In fact, not only did she have an ideal spot for watching the war as it affected Lexington, but she somehow managed to gather huge amounts of specific information that would have astonished war departments on both sides of the conflict. In her increasingly small, tight handwriting, Frances recorded troop movements, number of wounded, illnesses, promotions, reassignments and other valuable information.

Some she gleaned from reading newspapers. Her family apparently made it their business to stay well informed. Since her father was appointed senior surgeon responsible for all the hospitals in Lexington, she had access to records on how many soldiers arrived and from where. Whenever casualties were expected, her father would know, and somehow Frances knew, too.

Frances Peter's father, Robert. *Courtesy of J. Winston Coleman Jr. Photographic Collection, Transylvania University.*

In addition, she clearly had keen powers of observation, noting details of every sort. Her sources of information could have included soldiers who stopped by to chat, servants who overheard plenty, street exchanges of rumors and gossip, news from visitors, letters from family and friends elsewhere and firsthand observations when she attended various local events. All this information gathering was from a young woman, only nineteen when the war began, according to a family member who in later years transcribed some of her journals. Furthermore, Frances suffered from epileptic seizures for which there was no known cure and questionable treatment options.

Frances made a serious effort to get her facts straight. When she was uncertain, she said so. When her information was probably rumor, she made a note of that, too. She identified Union commanders and provided details with diligent attention to what she could verify as truth. Perhaps every woman in the city did the same, keeping track of what happened, when and where. But whether or not other women kept such detailed information,

Frances is the one who left behind a solid record of what happened in and around Lexington during the Civil War. So, in a very real sense, she was Lexington's chronicler, saving for posterity the facts and figures of how the Civil War changed the face of the city and the lives of the citizens there.

Frances watched and recorded the war's progress as power shifted hands and as residents lined up fiercely with factional divisions. She knew when Union soldiers raided the home of Southern sympathizer Henrietta Morgan, whose six sons and two sons-in-law would all fight for the Confederacy. Frances watched for activity at the Morgan home, when letters came and went or when the best-known of the Morgan boys, John Hunt Morgan, showed up for a quick, sneak visit with Mom.

Watching the Morgan house seemed one of Frances's favorite pastimes. Though as neighbors the Peter family and the Morgan family had been on fine terms before the war, secession tore the neighborhood apart as surely as it tore the nation apart. The Peter family remained staunchly pro-Union, while the Morgans avidly stood for the South. Among other neighbors, the divide reached into their own households, tearing apart family loyalties as one member headed South and another went for the North.

Though Frances made an effort to be fair to both sides, her own personal sentiments seeped through on just about every page. She labeled the Southern sympathizers as "Secesh" and verbally celebrated whenever their hopes for a Confederate victory collapsed. She delighted in making waspish comments about not only Southern sympathizers but also about the Confederate forces themselves when they arrived in Lexington to briefly occupy the city.

At one point she commented that the "Rebels skeddaddled as usual." But when rumors warned the Confederates were on their way, she remarked that the "citizens were in the greatest excitement." Then she described Morgan's men: "They looked like the tag, rag and bobtail of the earth and as if they hadn't been near water since Fort Sumter fell." Furthermore, she added, "The secesh had said that when John Morgan came he would have such a welcome as he had never seen before. I confess I was disappointed."

When rumors spread that the Union forces were on their way to take back the city, Frances remarked, "The rebel officers seem to be in a very bad humor today." She could hardly wait for the Federal soldiers to retake the city: "I hope it will not be long before the union troops whip these scamps here, for at the rate they are proceeding now they will strip us of everything we have. Lexington is almost ruined now." She was not one to mince words and said, "We are all very tired of the southern Confederacy."

As Frances noticed, the Southern sympathizers were packing their bags and taking down their Confederate flags. "The secesh wear very long faces," she noted with evident pleasure. Vehemently pro-Union, Frances declared, "I don't see how any one could look on our camps and think how many thousands of men have been driven from their homes by this war, suffering cold and hardship, and yet have any sympathy for the rebels who have brought all this on the country!" But she understood as well how vital Lexington and the entire state was to both sides. She said, "Kentucky is too valuable a state to the secesh for them to leave any stone unturned to get her."

Though Frances and her family were solid Union supporters, they weren't always so sure about Abraham Lincoln. She referred to the president in a late 1863 entry: "We did not think much of him at first and he only got one vote in Lexington, but the more we see of him the better we like him." With her information network providing opinions, she said of the next upcoming election, "I know a good many people here will vote for him."

In several sections of her journals, Frances remarked on outbreaks of fires in Lexington, wondering whether an arsonist might have been at work. With a lighter touch, in a personal letter not included with her war journals, she wrote, "The good city of Lexington was thrown into a state of excitement yesterday evening by the arrival of the steam fire engine. It was taken to Cheapside and tried. We couldn't imagine at first what the strange rumbling noise could be. First we thought it was cavalry coming in, then we were sure it was artillery or a large baggage train. Yet it didn't sound exactly like either." She described how the town turned out to watch and celebrate; even the hospitalized soldiers showed up. Such was the town's excitement over the new fire engine that she said, "We would not have been at all surprised if they had set the courthouse or some of the churches on fire just to see what the engine could do."

Her moments of humor underscored the strains and stresses of living through a war, watching soldiers march back and forth through town and being aware of not just the war wounded under her father's medical supervision but the pervasive threat of disease running rampant through the ranks as well. Her wit and bold opinions slipped through on many of the tightly written pages she so carefully used to document what war meant to her, her family and her hometown.

Interestingly, Frances did not reveal much about herself. She didn't make mention of her own illness or any limitations it must have made to her life. She did not spend much time or effort discussing eligible young men, though there must have been abundant supplies with so many soldiers occupying the city for most of the war. She didn't talk much about her family and never about her own appearance, clothes or hobbies. A relative left behind a description of Frances, saying, "She was a talented, charming girl" and admitting that "Frank is very scathing in her comment." Just reading the journals, though, provides little about Frances as a person. In the papers collected from the family, her sketchbooks revealed her talent as an artist. Her report card of 1855 from the Sayre Female Institute showed excellent grades in composition, mathematics, English grammar, history, reading, spelling, writing and geography; her deportment was considered "most exemplary."

The journals themselves consist of eight small books. The first book is Frances's French lesson book, which partway through she converted into a war journal starting with the date Sunday, January 19, 1862. Her writing became tighter, utilizing every inch of space as the war progressed and paper became scarce. The other books were created by sewing together long, narrow sheets of medical supply forms with thread. Frances wrote her entries on the back of these sheets, filling page after page with military details and anecdotes, sometimes writing from edge to edge.

In contrast to Frances, who wrote faithfully in her war journals, friend and neighbor Miriam Gratz kept sporadic journal entries when the mood felt right, she found a pen that worked and she had something to say. Only one book of her journal survived in the collection of family papers that includes Frances Peter's work. Miriam promised at the end of the journal kept with the Peter papers that she would end that book and begin another. Whether she did or not, only that one remains in the University of Kentucky Special Collections.

Miriam, like Frances, began in a marbleized notebook, with random blots and cross outs as well as marginal notes such as this one: "I know I am in love with the first lieutenant of the battery." Miriam's journal sounds like the diary of a young, single girl. Though she made frequent reference to the war, her interests often focused as much on who had gone off to fight, how each one looked in his uniform and whether he would write or not.

Her entries were sporadic, which she freely admitted: "I cannot say much for my promise of writing often, for instead of writing the next day I put it off until the next month, and that month passed and part of the following one." On August 24, 1861, Miriam remarked about having had a "delightful time" on a visit that was cut short due to the "death of my dear darling brother Cary." She went on to say, "He fell gallantly defending his country's flag on the blood stained fields of Springfield. Almost every paper is filled with accounts of the gallant little captain and a camp in the Southern part of Missouri was named in honor of his heroic behavior." Her fallen brother died fighting for the Union, and later she would share the details of his funeral: "This has been a bad week. Cary's body arrived Tuesday evening and his funeral took place yesterday." Though their father preferred no parade, Miriam explained that the Union men came anyway, "to show their respect for his memory and their love for the cause in which he fell…and my darling was buried with all the military pomp possible."

Touched in such a terribly personal way, still Miriam chose a chatty style for much of what she wrote, writing at one point, "Hurra I have at last through great difficulty got a good pen, and today for a great wonder feel like writing, although what I shall say still remains a mystery to me." Often she seemed to prefer cheerful personal items to actual war news. She said, "There are no boys in town[,] all have gone off either to the South or to this camp (Camp Robinson)." She added, "They have separate grounds for drilling infantry and cavalry, and all are enjoying themselves."

She remarked on young men she knew and had grown up with, making comments such as, "Will Dudley has gone to the Southern Army, he ought to be ashamed." Still she skipped days and even weeks, saying, "Some time has passed since I last wrote and civil war has broken out in Kentucky[;] almost every day for two weeks Soldiers have passed through…Several of these regiments brought with them some sick and the ladies have been very busy attending to their wants."

Seeing the sick soldiers apparently sent her thoughts to a certain young man she had mentioned often, finally admitting, "Why couldn't I have confessed the whole; and bravely say the truth about it, in other words I was in love with him." And when the young man in question left for the war, he came to say goodbye, and she lamented that with others present, "we had no opportunity to say much. He asked me to pray for him." She added that "he kissed my hand and looked very sad."

Though she recounted a selection of anecdotes and noted when local residents or family friends died, Miriam's focus was usually more personal than Frances's. Miriam saw the war as it affected her and her friends more than in its historical context. Her account simply stopped without lasting resolution. Frances seemed more inclined to consider herself a representative of her city and her state. She reported war news in detail, expecting that someday her words would fill in the gaps for generations to come who had not experienced the War Between the States.

Her feelings and opinions came across strongly. She was deeply involved emotionally, yet she strived for fairness in much of what she wrote. Unfortunately, some of her writing carried racist tones, which were, in fact, more common among Union supporters than many now realize. Still, she did her best to report the facts, to communicate the impact of the war on the lives of Lexingtonians and to be a witness to history all around her.

Speculating on how soon the war would end, Frances wrote at one point, "Won't it seem strange to have no war and no soldiers to look at. It will be extremely uninteresting." But for Frances Peter, the war ended on August 5, 1864, when she died as a result of an epileptic seizure. She did not live to see the war's end. Or learn of Abraham Lincoln's assassination. Or see the end of slavery and the rebuilding of a nation.

What she left behind is a rich legacy of one young woman's eyewitness account of a dreadful and bitter war, the changes it wrought on her hometown and a final glimpse into a way of life that would end forever. Not unlike Anne Frank, who would many years later record her youthful life in hiding from war and terror, Frances Peter died too young to develop her talents and abilities to their fullest and discover where life might have taken her. But her words have the power to take her readers into the heart of the Civil War in Lexington.

Chapter 14

Saving the Stars and Stripes

E lla Bishop must have been one feisty young woman. When the Confederate soldiers marched into Lexington in September 1862 to occupy the city for several weeks, young Ella defied the enemy to stand up for what she believed.

While young men like Cary Gratz willingly died to defend the flag of their country—the Stars and Stripes of the United States—the women mostly stayed home to care for their families, supported the troops by organizing fundraisers, wrote letters to encourage their men and even sewed flags to hang from homes and businesses. In her war journal, Miriam Gratz described how she sewed a regimental flag to present to one of the commanders stationed in Lexington.

Ella took her staunch pro-Union sentiments another giant step further. When the Confederacy claimed Lexington as its own, the invading troops tore down those American flags wherever they found them. Southern sympathizers eagerly broke out their Confederate flags to fly them from houses and public buildings. Meanwhile, the occupation army showed its disdain for the Union by mistreating the flags it pulled down around the city.

When Ella spotted the rowdy troops dragging flags in the streets of Lexington, she boldly stepped up and asked for one of the large flags. Thinking she sympathized with them, the Confederate soldiers handed over the American flag, and Ella, by some accounts, hurried home with her prize. When the occupying troops discovered that teenage Ella was not a

Southern sympathizer, supposedly they tracked her down to get back that flag. Ignoring the danger to herself, Ella reportedly refused to relinquish the precious flag and wrapped it around herself, telling the soldiers she would not give it up no matter what they said or did.

So, young Ella Bishop faced down the invading enemy with as much courage and boldness as any loyal soldier on a battlefield. The city must have been abuzz over Ella's actions. Frances Peter briefly noted Ella's exploit in her war journal: "Miss Ella Bishop was standing by when they took it [the flag] down and she asked them to give it to her. They thought she was a secesh and did so and she started to go home. Some one called to the rebels and told them she was Union so they sent a squad of men to her house to get the flag but she wouldn't give it up."

Later, Union soldiers would tell her story in letters sent home from the Bluegrass, where they were billeted after the Confederate occupancy ended. An account in *Old Houses of Lexington* by C. Frank Dunn discussed Ella's home, Cherry Grove, and her father, Purnell Bishop, who dealt in china and glassware. Dunn mentioned what he called a "charming bit of romance" about the home and the Bishop family. By Dunn's account, the "beautiful daughter" of the family, Ella, was outside the home while Confederate troops marched past. Dunn explained that troops "were constantly marching or riding past this place." He then went on to describe Ella catching sight of "a captured Federal flag," which she asked for and was quickly given, perhaps in admiration for her youthful attractiveness. By Dunn's telling, Ella then gave a cheer for Abe Lincoln and kept the flag wrapped firmly around herself. Dunn further remarked, "The officer—Captain Ransom—so admired her 'spunk'—and also her beauty—that he returned to Lexington after the war, married her and located in Cincinnati, where they reared a family."

A plaque affixed to a portrait of the young lady (on display at the Waveland Museum in Lexington) reads "Ella Bishop 1845–1926 Union Heroine of Lexington 1862 Born Lexington—Died Cincinnati Married Capt. E.P. Ransom 1863." So clearly, since the war didn't end until April 1865, she apparently did not wed a Confederate officer at the end of the war. Letters of the period indicate that Captain Ransom served the Union army as post commissary. Whether the Confederates she defied admired or respected her is unclear. They did, it seems, allow her to keep the flag she defied them to get. However romantic as Dunn's account might be with a Confederate officer returning for her at war's end, other accounts confirm that this audacious Union supporter married a man fighting on the same side.

Ella's heroism appeared in a newspaper notice in the *Lexington Observer and Reporter* in November 1862 with a brief summary of her bold behavior:

> *A very high compliment is paid to an estimable young lady of our city in a general order by Gen. G. Clay Smith, which we publish in another column. Miss Ella Bishop richly deserves every word that official paper contains. When Morgan's men made their last dash through our streets this noble young lady snatched from their grasp a beautiful flag, which they had torn from a corner building, and, waving it at them, held on to it in defiance of their efforts to get it from her until their departure.*

The newspaper also published the general's words of praise about Ella's loyalty. In an order lauding the young lady, Brigadier General G. Clay Smith designated the area headquarters to be named in her honor, Camp Ella Bishop. The Union general described how the enemy had thoroughly mistreated the American flag, "the banner we are so willing to defend." According to the general, "They trailed it in the dust and trampled it under their unhallowed feet and shouted it should wave no more over the city of Lexington, the state of Kentucky." The general then went on to describe "their hellish reveling and traitorous shouts" before turning his attention to Ella, calling her a "bold and patriotic, yet beautiful and modest lady scarcely eighteen years of age, one of Kentucky's proudest daughters." He explained that she acted with "undaunted courage" and "dared them to touch it with their polluted hands."

The general declared, "As an humble evidence therefore of respect and admiration for such patriotism and worthy example this camp shall bear the name of that young lady, 'Ella Bishop.'" So to commemorate her courage and heap honor on this determined and dedicated Unionist, the camp was called by her name. Not only did she enjoy having a camp named for her, but she also somehow gained a husband during the process, marrying E.P. Ransom and living with him at or near the camp while he served as commissary of subsistence, "assigned to duty as depot commissary of this post," according to the Official Records of the War Department. Her husband was later appointed "chief commissary of the District of Central Kentucky," according to those same War Department records.

Few other details about Ella's camp are readily available, but a number of accounts place Union soldiers in and around Lexington and the region during the war. Frances Peter described the daily comings and goings of Union soldiers, many of whom stayed in tents on the grounds in front of her home at what is now Gratz Park in downtown Lexington. Frances even sketched her neighborhood, showing Transylvania located at the top of her drawing, her house to the right, the Gratz home to the left just above the Hunt Morgan house on the same side and the troop tents in the center. In addition, a corner home on the right served as headquarters for officers.

Miriam Gratz in her war journal mentioned sick or wounded soldiers being scattered around town in a number of buildings, including a factory belonging to her father, Benjamin Gratz, a strong Union supporter. Other reports place Federal troops at the courthouse, on the grounds at Ashland (Henry Clay's former home) and at the old fairgrounds (which is the current location of the University of Kentucky). Many buildings were put to use as hospitals or prisons for captured enemy soldiers. From some reports, it sounds as if Lexington had become practically a fortress, suggestive of the importance and value placed on holding the city and the state for the Union cause.

Frances Peter spent much time noting which units were situated nearby, how many troops passed through the city and how many sick or wounded men arrived to receive care at the city's assorted medical locations. Though Lexington suffered few of the damages and indignities of other occupied communities or battle scenes, the city definitely felt the evidence of warfare, with soldiers drilling or patrolling throughout the community neighborhoods.

And though bold young Ella evidently lived the remainder of her life away from Lexington, her life certainly was shaped by her actions that one day when she chose to defy armed soldiers to protect the flag of her country. And her memory lives on in this tale of courage and determination in the face of threat and danger.

Chapter 15

The Homefront

When John Hunt Morgan rode triumphantly into his hometown, Lexington, in September 1862 as the Confederacy occupied the city, his heart must have lifted with great joy at the welcome he and his men received. Crowds turned out to greet them. Everywhere Union flags had been rapidly removed, and Confederate flags flew in their place. Believing that Lexington would gladly welcome the presence of Confederate forces and turn out with great enthusiasm, Morgan must have felt vindication. He'd assured his superiors that Lexington and all of Kentucky would respond if the Confederacy moved in boldly.

The welcome that day in the heart of Bluegrass country certainly reassured Morgan that it was only a matter of time before the entire city and state joined the Southern cause. Women mobbed him and his men, making them warmly welcome. Children thronged around, eagerly part of the excitement. Men turned out, as well, but perhaps not as enthusiastically as Morgan might have hoped, because by the end of the Confederate occupation of Lexington, few men joined up to fight, far fewer than Morgan had expected. It was the women of the Bluegrass who gave their gracious support.

According to Ranck in the *History of Fayette County*, when General Kirby Smith and his Southern troops entered the city, he and his men were greeted by "bands playing and colors flying…and were welcomed with smiles and shouts and waving of handkerchiefs by the delighted Southern sympathizers of the place, who, with hosts of men, women and children from all the surrounding counties, crowded the sidewalks." Morgan and his men were "met with a perfect storm of shouts and congratulations from their neighbors and relatives and friends, who crowded against the sides of the horses in the eagerness of their welcome." Morgan felt his spirit soar at the wonderful excitement of their greeting.

Ranck further described ladies "fluttering little Confederate flags, making every conceivable demonstration of delight, and pouring out their long-suppressed feelings to their heart's content." Additionally, "Everybody wanted to shake hands with Morgan; everybody wanted to shake hands with Duke, and everybody wanted to shake hands with everybody else in the command." Yes, Lexington turned out to welcome Morgan and his men. That was their home. That was where their wives and sweethearts, mothers and daughters waited for many of them. These were Kentucky boys, and Kentucky gladly took them in. But the warm welcome did not translate into signing up to fight for the Rebel cause.

As Kirby Smith later realized, the welcome was much more heavily female than male, with the men being more guarded in their response. The women of Lexington opened their hearts and their homes to these young men. But Lexington was not Confederate territory, no matter how glad the women might be to see their men safely among them again.

John Hunt Morgan received a hero's welcome because his exploits attracted admiration and excitement. Known as a chivalric hero, he drew fans and fluttered hearts. Admired for his gallantry and boldness, a sort of knight in shining armor, a dashing adventurer, John Morgan found himself the center of attention. In many cases, women so admired him that they used their sewing scissors to snip hairs from his horse's tail or mane. Everyone wanted to see him, shake his hand, touch him and be near him. In a time of war, death and grief, he was a shining star, an emblem of hope. Women came close to worshipping him, and men swore loyalty to him, at least those who chose to join up and fight under his leadership.

The women of Lexington felt a special bond—Morgan belonged to their city. Besides, most of the men who rode with him were Kentucky boys, and Kentucky cared for its own. The women made sure the soldiers were well fed, buying out the stores to provide the best they could offer. Lexington women hand-sewed regimental flags and made shirts for the soldiers who, many of them, wore virtual rags. Baking cakes, buying sweets, bringing flowers for the troops, the women turned out to show their loving support of their men.

Hunt Morgan home. *Courtesy of Barton Battaile Collection, Lexington Public Library.*

During the Confederate occupation of Lexington, the women of the city gave their dedication and devotion to the young men who had come home for such a brief time. But it wasn't just the Southern sympathizers who turned out to support their men. Union women did the same. When Morgan and his men moved out of Lexington, never to occupy the city again, women all over town pulled down those Confederate flags and flew the Stars and Stripes again. Shutters that had remained tightly shut during the Confederate occupation opened wide again to welcome the Union troops as they moved back into Lexington.

Throughout most of the war, it would be Union sympathizers who sustained those young men stationed among them. Union women held charity events to pay for goods and supplies for wounded soldiers. Dances, plays and musicals all attracted the local young people, as well as the officers stationed in town, and the women planned and ran events throughout the war years. Frances Peter often reported on the events held, how successful they were and what happened at the festivities. She wrote of the Aid Society and how actively the group of ladies worked to help provide for hospital patients. The fundraisers were great fun for everyone, but they served a serious purpose.

Local women made bandages, sewed for the men, prepared and delivered meals, visited the patients and generally ministered to their needs. Miriam Gratz wrote in her brief journal, "I have been very busy attending to the sick soldiers as all the sick of one regiment (Ohio 14th) are at our factory." Again she noted, "Was also up to see the hospital for the sick." With her favorite young man gone off to war, Miriam wrote, "I have devoted myself to the sick soldiers." Miriam noted that many locations around town had been converted into hospital facilities, such as the Masonic lodge, the college dormitories and the jail.

Miriam also wrote about three hundred sick soldiers housed in a local hospital, and she added that another fifty were in the college dormitory, which was being used as a hospital. Taking the whole thing very personally, Miriam noted that there was a "terrible battle" and "many of 'our boys' took part in it." She also mentioned the benefit events for aid to wounded or sick soldiers, and she wrote of helping out by sewing for the soldiers. She referred to her worry about the weather, writing, "If that weather lasts very long I would not be surprised if we had many sick soldiers." And though she sounded almost exasperated when she wrote, "We live in the middle of soldiers," still she, like so many Lexington women of all ages, took an interest in the welfare of "our boys."

And for those women who had loved ones taken prisoner, they frequently sent packages of homemade foodstuff and whatever else they could think of to bring a touch of home to bleak and often dangerous prisons. Men taken captive suffered, often not having sufficient food, warm clothing and adequate bedding. Prisons were often severely overcrowded and sometimes badly run. Many women like Henrietta Morgan, who had several sons taken captive and held as prisoners of war, made every effort to visit their sons or husbands. The women did their best to make living conditions in those prisons as survivable as possible.

As with sons in current-day circumstances, some of the prisoners wrote home asking for what they needed. Henrietta had several letters from her son Thomas while he was a prisoner. And like many sons in just about any time period, her son let her know exactly what he needed. One letter in the

University of Kentucky Special Collections read, "I am entirely out of a change of clothing…Will you please have (me) some flannel shirts made after the pattern of linen ones. I do not want any white shirts at all. Also under shirts. Drawers. And socks. I should like to have my clothes which I left in Lexington last summer." What mother of sons hasn't heard similar requests?

Then another letter Henrietta received from her prisoner son read, "I have no particular amount of money to ask from you. Whatever you may send will be most acceptable." This was not so very different from letters sent these days from sons or daughters away from home. The women at home sent whatever they could to help sons, fathers, husbands and brothers feel as comfortable as possible while away from home. Some even tried to get their family members released from prison, as with Confederate agent George Sanders's wife, who wrote a letter that found its way to Jefferson Davis's desk asking for her son's release from prison. Though Davis wrote that he could not obtain her son's release, he made sure that she received her son's pay. Unfortunately, her son later died.

Prison life was highly hazardous, as many of those wives, mothers, sisters and daughters knew. Sickness raged through populations of weakened soldiers who probably didn't have enough to eat or warm enough clothing before they got to the prison. Some prisons were notorious for mistreatment, and some prisoners refused to cooperate with rules, making their lives even more uncertain. Medicines were hard to come by, as were many basic supplies, which added to the risks of prison life.

Besides letters home from captive sons in need of undergarments, women kept up a steady stream of encouraging letters to their men fighting on the battlefield. Under a flag of truce, letters could be sent from one side to the other even during lulls on the fighting front. Sometimes those letters had to be censored to avoid any sensitive information changing hands. But many women managed to get around the censors by using codes or by sending their mail by secret couriers.

Frances Peter, while watching the Morgan house, suspected those secret couriers were showing up at night, hiding out and slipping past guards. In one journal entry, Frances noted, "Someone was arrested at Mrs. Morgan's this evening." That someone could easily have been a spy or secret courier. Henrietta Morgan's home seemed a focal point for suspicion, since she had several sons fighting for the Confederacy at any given time; all six of her boys were solid Southern supporters. Another time, Frances observed that Mrs. Morgan's house was searched and a guard set, though no one was found evidently. Frances also pointed out in a journal entry that five "secesh" ladies were arrested for "expressing treasonable sentiments," and when they were threatened with being sent south to join their "dear rebel friends," the ladies all preferred to stay put, go to jail instead and take an oath of allegiance. Frances underscored the apparent fact that there were "too many traitors in our midst."

Miriam, too, kept a watchful eye on neighbor Henrietta Morgan's household, mentioning "quite an exciting scene" at the Morgan home. She described how a boy carrying letters back and forth for the Rebels was caught, arrested and escaped. He then "took refuge at Mrs. Morgan's" until soldiers arrived to track him down. At that point, a servant led the soldiers around to the side of the house, where they caught ladies of the household assisting the spy to get away. Clearly, watching the Morgan house provided fascinating entertainment and plenty of excitement for the neighbors.

Letters from the women at home often arrived crammed with local news and even news from the battlefields. A letter in the University of Kentucky Special Collections files written to James B. Clay, son of the famed statesman Henry Clay, held news from home. His wife filled eight pages with her deepest thoughts, ranging from her Christian faith to her hopes for news of friends and family far from home. She wrote of the death of Henrietta Morgan's son Thomas: "He was killed at Lebanon, shot through the heart. His last words as he fell back into Cal Morgan's arms, were 'Oh brother Cally they have killed me.' His death is a terrible blow to his poor mother."

Her letter went on to give details of a Confederate officer taken prisoner, brought to Lexington and held in the former slave jail. She expressed worry over "Jimmy," about not knowing where he was or what had happened to him and the anxiety she felt not being able to learn what had happened to him. Her plight was not so very different from the situation of so many of the women left behind to worry and wonder. Rumors flew, and no one could be sure what was truth and what was false.

Many women left behind gathered as much information as they could, tried to keep up their courage and dedicated themselves to helping where they could, all while caring for homes and children. Other women stayed as near their men as possible, traveling with the troops when they were able to without putting themselves in danger. Basil Duke wrote to his wife, Tommie, in a letter now in the University of Kentucky Special Collections, letting her know how he was doing after an injury: "I am not seriously hurt but much weakened by loss of blood and the concussion of the brain caused by a ball passing so near it." Though he expressed doubts about her safety, he couldn't resist commenting, "I would get well directly if I had you to nurse me," and he said, "I am very anxious to get to some point where you can be with me, and I must stand in another day if I do not hear from you." Besides, he missed their little boy.

Duke's wife made every effort to be there for him, just as John C. Breckinridge's wife did. Mary Breckinridge got the nickname of "mother" to the troops. She stayed as close as she could and did whatever she was able to do to make life more tolerable not just for her husband but also for the young Kentucky boys who fought with him.

And when needed, Lexington women stayed beside the dying to bring comfort in their final moments. When John Morgan led his raid on the Union troops at Ashland, he was forced to leave his dying relative behind when he moved on. The mortally wounded man spent his final hours with Morgan's mother, resting in her home until the end came. The women cared for the sick and dying and then arranged for funerals to honor them. And when at last the war was over, women welcomed their men back home again.

Some even went out of their way to mend the brokenness that had torn apart homes, families and neighborhoods. According to Catherine Peter Evans, the Peter family vividly recalled the day "after the war was over, when Mrs. Morgan, in deep mourning, drove in her carriage to Mrs. Peter's country home, Winton, to cry on Mrs. Peter's shoulder, and to beg her to forget all past prejudices and be friends again."

The fighting was done. The hatred hopefully fallen away. The grief still to be lived with, and old friends to join together in their losses to find hope for the future.

Chapter 16

Conspiracies

Side by side the Lincolns enjoyed their evening at the theater. Mary snuggled close, and they held hands. They'd never been closer or more at ease. The war had ended. The long nightmare was over. Now they could begin a new life together, a new era for the country they loved. Their time in the White House could only get better now. The future appeared bright and full of hope for them both.

But not for John Wilkes Booth. He'd prepared the way, scouted the presidential box, planned carefully and now was his moment. The time for revenge had come, and he was ready. He stepped into the theater box and into history, the man who killed President Abraham Lincoln. Booth fired his derringer close to Lincoln's head, behind the left ear and directly into that remarkable brain. Then Booth grappled with the Lincolns' guest Major Rathbone, slashing the other man's arm before making his spectacular leap from the presidential box onto the stage below, breaking his leg in the process.

Booth's action was not a solitary act. He'd planned the evening thoroughly, but his team failed him. The plan called for the death of the president, yes, but it also called for the death of the vice president and the secretary of state. Killing those three was calculated to throw the government into chaos and potentially open the door for a Southern revival. If the Federal government collapsed, then perhaps the Confederacy could step into the gap and regain strength and purpose—likely Booth's thinking. Nothing worked quite according to plan.

Above: Lincoln assassinated. Published in *Harper's Weekly*, April 29, 1865. *Courtesy of Douglas W. Bostick*.

Left: John Wilkes Booth. Published in *Harper's Weekly*, April 29, 1865. *Courtesy of Douglas W. Bostick*.

First, the original plan called for a kidnapping rather than an assassination plot. But the kidnapping failed, through no fault of their own—Lincoln had not showed up where he was supposed to be—so the team switched to murder instead. Of the conspirators, only Booth reached his goal. Many of the rest of his team were rounded up, brought to trial, convicted and punished; four of the accused were hanged. Booth made a brief escape before being cornered in a barn, shot and killed. He would never take the stand and testify. He would never accuse anyone else of being behind the whole plan.

There is no proof that anyone else other than Booth and his team was involved in the death of Lincoln. But throughout the Union, suspicion stirred and solidified quickly into the belief that the Confederacy had set up the whole thing. Fingers pointed at known Confederate agents, including a man with a Lexington connection, Thomas H. Hines, whose parents lived in the Bluegrass and who had designed the escape plan that got John Hunt Morgan out of an Ohio penitentiary. Hines was a Confederate who later historians would place at the center of what was known as the Northwest Conspiracy for the South, a plan to release prisoners of war and use them to attack Northern cities.

Confederate leaders were also sought in connection with the murder of Lincoln, including Jefferson Davis, whose name topped the list. Davis was a wanted man, and once Booth was dead, the Union forces focused their frustration and rage on the Confederate president. Davis and his cabinet fled, at differing paces and in a range of directions. Some of them escaped the country, never to return again. Others slipped back into the United States quietly. A few waited for an amnesty to allow them to return.

Historians split their vote on whether Davis had any involvement in the death of Lincoln. James Swanson in his book *Bloody Crimes* insisted that Davis knew nothing about any of it. Said Swanson, "Davis did not know John Wilkes Booth and had not sent him to kill Lincoln." Swanson did state that though Davis had no knowledge of the plan, "Booth had met with Confederate secret agents in Montreal, Canada," and that Booth had then assembled his killing team as well as an escape plan that involved Confederate networking.

By William A. Tidwell's reckoning in his book *Come Retribution*, "It was widely believed in the North that the Confederate government might have

Ulric Dahlgren. Published in *Harper's Weekly*, March 26, 1864. *Courtesy of Douglas W. Bostick.*

been involved in the assassination of Lincoln." He did acknowledge that any evidence in support of Confederate leadership being involved was largely circumstantial, though he detected plenty of hints that pointed in the direction of Davis and his government. The whole thing began with a man named Ulric Dahlgren, a Union officer who set out to rescue Federal captives in a Richmond prison. Everyone knew by then that prisoners were mistreated in many prisons, poorly fed, vulnerable to disease and starvation.

Dahlgren was supposed to take a force in to set the prisoners free, but his assignment failed, and he was killed in the process. According to Confederate sources, Dahlgren carried papers on him that indicated his mission included murdering Davis and his cabinet, as well as destroying the city of Richmond and civilians who might be in the way. This was not gentlemanly warfare. This was, to the South's way of thinking, savagery and barbarism. It was unspeakable. The contents of Dahlgren's orders were made public, and the South rose in indignant rage.

From that moment on, anything in the way of retaliation was fair game, and what was called "black flag" operations supposedly began. Whether the black ops were approved by Davis or not is under debate, but the existence of black ops seems fairly well known. Kentuckian Luke Pryor Blackburn's alleged attempt at biological warfare by spreading yellow fever in Northern population centers falls under this category. Other alleged plots involved burning cities such as New York, stirring up internal revolt wherever possible, loosing Confederate prisoners to loot and pillage Northern cities and a range of other possibilities.

Dahlgren's friends and family denied that the young officer carried any such orders. His men and officers claimed never to have heard of such orders, which would have been their job to implement. His family insisted that the signature on the orders was not his and that the name was even misspelled. Critics of the Confederacy suspected that the orders were forged, a justification for starting a black flag program.

When it came time to capture and try Davis, nobody could prove any of the suspicions. No paperwork existed to link him or his cabinet to the suspected plots. Nothing connected Davis or the Southern agents with Booth's assassination plans. Certainly, nothing came to light that could prove the case in a court of law. Davis denied any knowledge of the plot to kill Lincoln and wanted a day in court. Instead, he was turned loose on bail and never prosecuted for anything.

John Wilkes Booth, Jefferson Davis, George N. Sanders. In the summation of the Honorable John Bingham, special judge advocate in the Lincoln assassination conspiracy trial, these three names were listed in succession, along with several others, as confederates in the assassination of President Abraham Lincoln. George N. Sanders was listed alongside the president of the Confederate States of America and the known assassin of the president of the United States. Who was Sanders to have achieved such attention?

George Nicholas Sanders, born in Lexington, Kentucky, grew up in Carroll County among influential minds on both sides of his family and was a driven but unorthodox man. He proposed to his wife, Anna, sight unseen, even relying upon Henry Clay, whom he barely knew, for a recommendation to her family. Along with his father, he participated in a small local meeting designed to force the issue of the annexation of Texas into the presidential election. Only the eventual winner Polk seized the opportunity the issue presented, and men such as Henry Clay were arguably hindered in their own bids by the issue. After his success influencing the election, Sanders was inspired to move to New York City and take up the pursuit of business and political power more directly.

Sanders soon became a leader with a progressive wing of the Democratic Party, Young Democracy, which included Stephen Douglas among its supporters and beneficiaries. Though Sanders and YD failed to promote Douglas to the highest office, their support did aid President Pierce, who appointed Sanders consul general in London in return. But Sanders only held the position a brief three months before his public associations with European revolutionaries led the Senate to deny him confirmation.

George N. Sanders. Published in *Harper's Weekly*, August 26, 1865. *Courtesy of Douglas W. Bostick.*

During the war, Sanders worked for the Confederate States of America navy, arranging for construction of ships overseas. A courier service he operated between Richmond, England and France also involved his sons Lewis and Reid, but Reid was captured and imprisoned. Anna Sanders wrote a letter personally to Jefferson Davis seeking aid for her son—not the only correspondence between the Sanders family and Davis, as seen in the George Sanders letters—and though she received a response from the CSA secretary of war that Reid could not be exchanged and Jefferson Davis had his secretary arrange that Anna got Reid's salary, her son died in prison.

George Sanders returned to North America and joined Confederate agents in Canada. During this time, he was familiar with Tom Hines, the leader of Confederate covert operations in Canada and the North, an association that perhaps led to some belief that Sanders had met with

Booth, given the strong resemblance between Booth and Hines. Sanders also befriended Confederate commissioners in Canada, most notably Clement C. Clay. Author James Horan and others even suggest that the famous bank robberies by Confederate agents and resulting trial were a result of Sanders forging the signature of Clay for authorization while Hines, who had refused, was away. According to Horan, Hines did not like Sanders and his methods, and the Confederate mastermind even collected clippings of Sanders for years.

To this day, there are those who believe George Nicholas Sanders was not only involved in the assassination but perhaps even had a controlling hand in it. Sanders had a reputation for supporting the assassination of tyrants. After Sanders lost the consulship, author Peter Bridges noted, "Sanders stayed on in London for some months, and in October 1854 the former consul issued a long 'Address to the People of France,' calling on them to revolt against Napoleon III and reestablish a republic." Conspiracy theorists also link him to a shadowy group, the Knights of the Golden Circle, which was revived and reorganized in Lexington by five unknown men and grew into a large network nationwide. Other alleged members included Davis, Booth and the James brothers, famous outlaws and friends to Confederate general Jo Shelby. Sanders's author friend Victor Hugo also had ties to a related secret organization.

While in Canada, Sanders did apparently work for peace, as well, arranging a peace conference at Niagara Falls along with Horace Greeley. That conference failed, of course, and his friendship with Greeley, many say, damaged the latter's political career later in his life. Such was often the way with Sanders, a man characterized by great ambitions and sullied perceptions. While he had no official authority or role in Canada for the Confederacy, he inserted himself into operations there so evidently that he earned his place among a dozen men accused of conspiracy in the assassination of Lincoln, and he was one of five men, headed by Jefferson Davis, excluded from the benefits of President Johnson's Proclamation of Amnesty. A reward was issued for Sanders's arrest, and while he was not proven guilty of such treason as many believed him guilty, like many other Confederate notables, Sanders would remain in exile for many years because of his notoriety. George Nicholas Sanders returned to New York in 1872, some eleven years after leaving the country. He died a year later.

Chapter 17

Journey's End

Massive trees spread arms of blooming branches overhead. Grassy rolling hillocks and narrow winding roadways lead through acres of peaceful venues. Tiny star-like flowers sprinkle through the lush grass, and clear ponds ripple beneath ducks and geese that winter there. No place in Lexington offers as lovely and gentle a welcome as the Lexington Cemetery, especially for those who rest here after lives deeply shaken and permanently altered by a bloody and terrible war.

There's no mistaking Henry Clay's final resting place. The Great Compromiser. Harry of the West. The Sage of Ashland. Statesman and diplomat. Perhaps the most honored and respected Kentuckian of his time. The monument to honor him towers 120 feet into the bright blue sky in the heart of the Bluegrass region. The larger-than-life statue of Henry Clay stands atop a graceful column, a reminder for all time of the man and his monumental efforts to save the unity of the nation he loved so fiercely and dreamt of someday leading.

His funeral was impressive, orchestrated by friends and admirers. A committee of esteemed citizens from his home city, including his friend Benjamin Gratz, traveled to Washington, D.C., after his death to bring back his remains to the Bluegrass, where he'd said he wished to be laid for his repose. According to Professor Ranck in the *History of Fayette County*, businesses closed, church bells tolled in mourning and the funeral train bringing his remains home was met everywhere along the way by grieving

Clay monument. *Courtesy of Library of Congress.*

crowds. The man who had hoped to be president of the United States stirred the hearts and spirits of the nation even in death.

When Clay's remains at last reached his home and funeral plans were completed, again according to Ranck, "crowds of people poured into Lexington by every avenue to the city...soon the largest crowd of people that had ever assembled in Lexington was gathered together." Ranck went on to describe the grand procession, the team of six matched white horses pulling the hearse, the speeches, bells and guns and a city draped in mourning. Though he was buried near his mother, Clay's remains were later moved to the elegant monument designed to honor his memory. At the time of his wife's death, in 1864, both were, as Ranck put it, "encased in a marble sarcophagus and placed permanently side by side in the chamber of the Clay Monument."

The statue itself would suffer the indignity of severe damage from a ferocious thunderstorm in July 1903 that lopped off the statue's head, leaving it partially buried in the ground below. Repairs were completed by 1910, but within months of the refurbishment, lightning again struck, shattering one arm and leg. This time the statue was supplied with a lightning rod to protect it from any further damages. One side note is the coincidental death of Henry Clay's audacious, aged cousin Cassius Clay within twenty-four hours of the statue's initial destruction.

Though the statue once towered high above any other structure in the city, modern expansion has left it less notable in the skyline. Still, the Honorable Henry Clay can be seen from quite a distance, his influence well remembered, his achievements still admired. And who knows what course the nation's history might have taken had he reached his dream to gain the presidency? The words carved into his sarcophagus say it all for him: "I can with unshaken confidence appeal to the divine arbiter for the truth of the declaration that I have been influenced by no impure purpose, no personal motive, have sought no personal aggrandizement but that in all my public acts, I have had a sole and single eye, and a warm devoted heart directed and dedicated to what in my best judgment I believe to be the true interest of my country."

The Civil War, which Henry Clay did all in his power to avert, devastated so many lives, left so many young men dead before their time and forever altered so many other lives even after it ended. Hundreds found their final rest in the peaceful environs of the Lexington Cemetery, returning to their heart's home to lie beneath the ground among the hallowed dead of both sides. Brothers beside brothers, neighbors near neighbors. For instance, two of Henry Clay's sons—Thomas, who firmly supported the Union, and James, who fled the country because of his Confederate sympathies—rest not far apart. Men who had fought one another on the field of battle now lie at peace in home soil.

John Hunt Morgan, who died before war's end, was honored among his fellow Confederates, mourned and buried twice before finally returning to his Bluegrass homeland. He and his brother Thomas, who also died before the war's end, lie side by side for their final rest. In the family plot, John Hunt Morgan's stone stands at the center, always his undisputed spot, surrounded by a doleful semicircle of those he loved and who loved him. His mother rests to his right side, his brother Thomas to his left and beyond Thomas lies their brother Francis Key. Each gravestone is marked, for each

John Hunt Morgan and family. *Authors' collection.*

of the Morgan boys, CSA. Every one of them fought for the South, and their markers tell the story.

And among the Morgan family lies a small marker to show the burial place for their lifelong servant, the woman who helped raise the boys and who, when set free, chose to stay with the family. Her name was Bouviette, and her marker reads "Ever Faithful." Not far from the Hunt Morgan plot rests Morgan's business partner, Sanders Bruce, who fought for the Union. Morgan's first wife, Bruce's sister Rebecca, and Morgan's infant son lie there, too. Near the Bruce plot lies the Gratz family section, where Miriam rests close by her brother Cary, who died fighting for the Union, and her father, who staunchly supported the Union.

Side by side in death as in their almost five decades of married life, Basil Wilson Duke and his Tommie, Henrietta Morgan Duke, share a single headstone, nothing showy or dramatic but clean and well tended, close by the man he so admired—brother-in-law, leader and friend John Hunt Morgan, fallen Hero of the South. And sometimes in the peaceful quiet

Basil W. and Tommie Duke. *Authors' collection.*

of the cemetery, someone places a small Confederate flag in front of the gravestone Duke and his beloved wife share. Their hearts were one, unified in life and in death, devoted to each other, to their family and to the cause they all shared.

Not far away, in the Todd family plot, rests the Southern contingent of Mary Todd Lincoln's family. The "Little Sister" Emilie whom Mary and Abraham so loved lies there among the Todds. Close to Emilie rest her children, including Katherine, who painted lovely portraits of Mary Lincoln and who also wrote a biography about Mary and her marriage to Abraham Lincoln.

Mary does not lie in the Lexington Cemetery with her birth family. She rests with her husband and sons in Springfield, Illinois. But her father and mother, her stepmother and other siblings lie in the Lexington Cemetery. Her stepmother honored Mary's half brothers who fought for the South with a marker that reads: "In memory of my boys Samuel B. Todd, David H. Todd, Alexander H. Todd, All Confederate soldiers." Even in death,

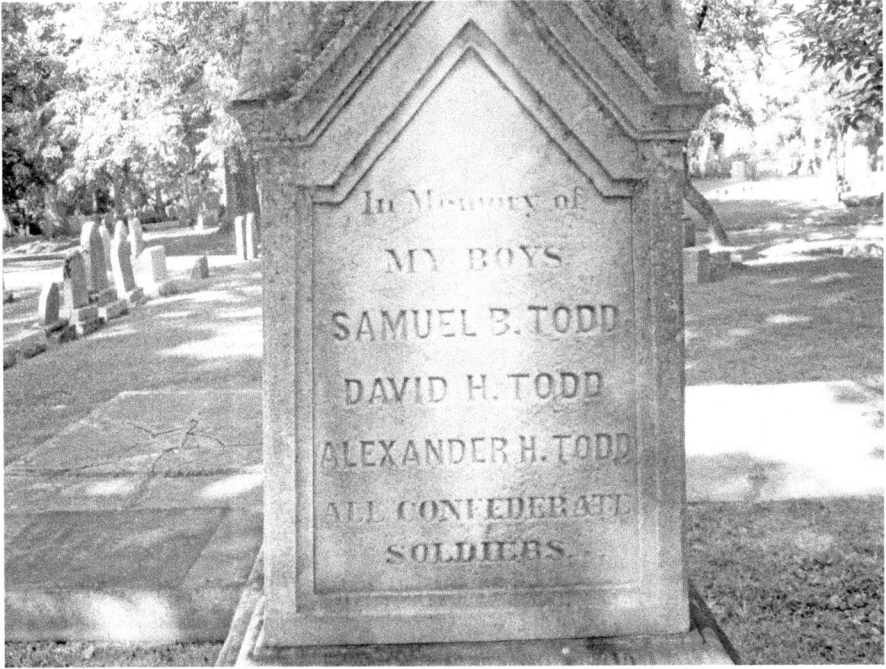

Todd family monument. *Authors' collection.*

Mary's family lies divided, the Confederate members in the Bluegrass, the Union members elsewhere.

Generals from both sides have found their journey's end at the Lexington Cemetery. Among them are Roger W. Hanson of the Orphan Brigade, Abraham Buford and Randall Gibson, all Confederates, as well as Gordon Granger, Union.

Without an understated cemetery marker to identify the spot, John Cabell Breckinridge's final resting place might never be noticed. No monument or ornate stone marks where he lies—a man who served as vice president of the United States, resigned a Senate seat, ran for president, led soldiers in battle and closed the conflict as Confederate secretary of war. Not a word of it on his headstone—only his name and dates. Nothing more. In death as in life, an unassuming man of steadfast honor. The words on his stone are barely readable, and nearby trees shade the spot, making the stone even more difficult to read. His family surrounds him in death as they did in life. Beside him lies his precious wife, Mary, who stood by him through years of trouble and brokenness.

John C. Breckinridge and wife. *Authors' collection.*

In his exile from the nation he loved, John C. Breckinridge longed to return to his home, ached with the realization that he was estranged from his own people and missed the flag that had been his before the nation split apart. In the quiet spot where he has found rest from his life's journey, John C. Breckinridge has returned to his Bluegrass homeland, and in that peaceful corner, a small American flag stands by his marker in honor of his service to the United States of America. He had come home at last to stay.

Conclusion

A ccording to Cassius Clay, who was never accused of humility, he personally influenced President Lincoln in releasing the Emancipation Proclamation. Clay, who had earlier claimed to impress Lincoln with his fiery emancipation speeches, declared to Lincoln that Kentucky would not be lost to the Union if Lincoln went ahead with emancipation. As he explained it, he'd spent a quarter of a century preparing Kentucky for slavery to end, and no one would be taken by surprise. Lincoln issued the proclamation, Clay claimed a share of credit and the nation was forever changed.

How much actual credit goes to Cassius Clay can't be determined, but certainly a degree of credit for emancipation must go to Lincoln's "beau ideal" of a statesman, Lexington's Henry Clay. Lincoln confessed himself influenced by Henry Clay, even considering the possible merits of colonization as a solution for the slavery issue. And most certainly Henry Clay's deep passion for holding together the Union must have affected Lincoln, who himself stood firm, refusing to budge on his commitment to the Union. How could Lincoln, as much as he respected and admired Henry Clay, allow the nation to dissolve on his watch when Clay had given himself so fully to preserving the nation?

Wherever the credit may go, Lincoln changed the face of the nation by freeing the slaves and putting an end to the peculiar institution. He'd seen slavery in its darkest moments while visiting Lexington with his Bluegrass bride, Mary, where slave traders plied their trade, where slave auctions were the norm and where the whipping post stood as a painful reminder

Emancipation Proclamation.
Courtesy of Library of Congress.

Lincoln the Emancipator. *Courtesy of Library of Congress.*

of inequality. In his second inaugural address, Lincoln made his views unmistakably plain. Slavery was evil, and perhaps the bloody war came as some degree of atonement.

The war was indeed bloody. An estimated 620,000 men died, many of disease and dreadful living conditions, as well as of war wounds. A National Cemetery was established in Lexington, where an American flag honors the fallen Union war dead. Two monuments in the Lexington Cemetery honor the fallen Confederates, reminding visitors that men on both sides lost their lives fighting for what they believed was right.

The Bluegrass has not forgotten the fallen. John Hunt Morgan, hero for the Southern cause, is honored as a hometown boy who lost his life in the war. His statue can be seen at the old courthouse location, where he sits astride a stately mount as if ready to rush into battle. Nearby, a statue to honor John C. Breckinridge stands atop a column surrounded by plaques that list his history and accomplishments. He was a man whose life appeared destined for greater things. He'd already served as vice president and senator

National Cemetery in Lexington. *Authors' collection.*

Confederate soldier monument. *Authors' collection.*

Confederate memorial. *Authors' collection.*

Morgan equestrian statue.
Authors' collection.

John C. Breckinridge statue.
Authors' collection.

of the United States. He ran for president and then found himself caught up in the turmoil of the age, becoming a Confederate general and finally secretary of war for the Confederacy.

And at Transylvania University, two impressive paintings honor men whose lives were entangled with the university. Jefferson Davis soaked up learning and culture during his time at Transylvania. He made friends there who lasted him all his life and who would help shape the future of the nation. Henry Clay, statesman and presidential aspirant, served as teacher and trustee for the university, helping to shape future generations who then helped to lead the country through the war years and beyond.

Henry Clay monument. *Authors' collection.*

Henry Clay
campaign poster.
*Courtesy of Joseph
Murphy.*

Lexington played a role in the years before, during and after the Civil War, shaping the characters of men and women who provided leadership, influenced history and shaped the future of the nation. The United States would not be united without the efforts of some of these individuals who were in so many ways affected by the Bluegrass and their experiences there. Today, tourists browse through historic homes and museums. Collectors gather mementos such as election posters and campaign tokens as reminders of these men of power. Memorial ceremonies bring out descendants and visitors who remember the fallen.

Henry Clay campaign token. *Courtesy of Joseph Murphy.*

Lexington, Kentucky, indeed, served as a breeding ground of power, a cultural and educational center, a jumping-off place for political aspirations and a safe haven for those who finally returned to the heart of the Bluegrass at their journey's end.

Selected Bibliography

PUBLISHED BOOKS

Allardice, Bruce S., and Laurence Lee Hewitt, eds. *Kentuckians in Gray: Confederate Generals and Field Officers of the Bluegrass State*. Lexington: University Press of Kentucky, 2008.

Arnett, Larry L., Col. *Call to Arms: A Collection of Fascinating Stories, Events, Personalities and Facts About Kentucky's Military History*. Frankfort: Kentucky Publishing Co., 1995.

Baird, Nancy Disher. *Luke Pryor Blackburn: Physician, Governor, Reformer*. Lexington: University Press of Kentucky, 1979.

Baker, Jean H. *Mary Todd Lincoln, A Biography*. New York: W.W. Norton & Co., 1987.

Ballard, Michael B. *A Long Shadow: Jefferson Davis and the Final Days of the Confederacy*. Jackson: University Press of Mississippi, n.d.

Black, Robert B., Col. *Cavalry Raids of the Civil War*. Mechanicsburg, PA: Stackpole Books, 2004.

Bridges, Peter. *Pen of Fire: John Moncure Daniel*. Kent, OH: Kent State University Press, 2002.

Brooks, Eric. *Ashland: The Henry Clay Estate*. Charleston, SC: Arcadia Publishing, 2007.

Brown, Kent Masterson, ed. *The Civil War in Kentucky: Battle for the Bluegrass State*. Mason City, IA: Savas Publishing Co., 2000.

Brown, William Wells. *Clotel or the President's Daughter*. 1853. New edition, Armonk, New York: M.E. Sharpe, 1996.

———. *My Southern Home: or, The South and Its People*. 1880. Repr., New York: Negro Universities Press, 1969.

———. *Narrative of William Wells Brown, a Fugitive Slave. Written by Himself*. Boston: published at the Anti-Slavery Office, No. 25 Cornhill, 1847.

———. *The Negro in the American Rebellion: His Heroism and His Fidelity*. New York: Citadel Press, 1971.

Burton, Orville Vernon, ed. *The Essential Lincoln Speeches and Correspondence*. New York: Farrar, Straus and Girioux, 2009.

Clay, Cassius M. *The Life Memoirs, Writings, and Speeches of Cassius M. Clay, In Two Volumes*. Vol. 1. Cincinnati, OH: J. Fletcher Brennan & Co., 1886.

Clinton, Catherine. *Mrs. Lincoln, A Life*. New York: HarperCollins, 2009.

Coleman, J. Winston, Jr. *Slavery Times in Kentucky*. Chapel Hill: University of North Carolina Press, 1940.

Cooper, William J., Jr. *Jefferson Davis, American*. New York: Alfred A. Knopf, 2000.

Davenport, F. Garvin. *Ante-Bellum Kentucky: A Social History, 1800–1860*. N.p.: Mississippi Valley Press, 1943. Repr., Westport, CT: Greenwood Press Publishers, reprint 1983.

Davis, Varina. *Jefferson Davis, Ex-President of the Confederate States of America: A Memoir by His Wife*. 2 vols. New York: Bedford Co., Publishers, 1890.

Davis, William C. *Breckinridge: Statesman, Soldier, Symbol*. Baton Rouge: Louisiana State University Press, 1974.

————, ed. *Diary of a Confederate Soldier: John S. Jackman of the Orphan Brigade*. Columbia: University of South Carolina Press, 1990.

————. *The Orphan Brigade: The Kentucky Confederates Who Couldn't Go Home*. Garden City, NY: Doubleday & Co., 1980.

Duke, Basil. *History of Morgan's Cavalry*. Cincinnati, OH: Miami Printing & Publishing, 1867.

————. *Reminiscences of General Basil W. Duke*. Freeport, NY: Books for Libraries Press, 1911. Repr., 1969.

Dunn, C. Frank. *Old Houses of Lexington*. 2 vols. Typescript.

Emerson, Jason. *The Madness of Mary Lincoln*. Carbondale: Southern Illinois University Press, 2007.

Epstein, Daniel Mark. *The Lincolns: Portrait of a Marriage*. New York: Ballantine Books, 2009.

Farrison, William Edward. *William Wells Brown: Author and Reformer*. Chicago: University of Chicago Press, 1969.

Harrison, Lowell H. *The Civil War in Kentucky*. Lexington: University Press of Kentucky, 1975.

————, ed. *Kentucky's Governors*. Lexington: University Press of Kentucky, 1985, 2004.

————. *Lincoln of Kentucky*. Lexington: University Press of Kentucky, 2000.

Harrison, Lowell H., and James C. Klotter. *A New History of Kentucky*. Lexington: University Press of Kentucky, 1997.

Hattaway, Herman, and Richard E. Berringer. *Jefferson Davis, Confederate President*. Lawrence: University of Kansas Press, 2002.

Hay, Melba Porter, ed. *The Papers of Henry Clay. Vol. 10: Candidate, Compromiser, Elder Statesman, Jan. 1, 1844–June 29, 1852*. Lexington: University Press of Kentucky, 1991.

Helm, Katherine. *Mary, Wife of Lincoln*. New York: Harper & Brothers, Publishers, 1928.

Hollingsworth, Randolph. *Lexington: Queen of the Bluegrass*. Charleston, SC: Arcadia Publishing, 2004.

Holzer, Harold, and Joshua Wolf Shenk, eds. *In Lincoln's Hand: His Original Manuscripts with Commentary by Distinguished Americans*. New York: Bantam Books, 2009.

Horan, James D. *Confederate Agent: A Discovery in History*. New York: Crown Publishers, Inc., 1954.

Johnson, Isaac, a Former Slave. *Slavery Days in Old Kentucky*. Facsimile of 1901 ed. Canton, NY: Friends of the Owen D. Young Library & the St. Lawrence County Historical Association, 1994.

Jones, Edgar DeWitt. *The Influence of Henry Clay Upon Abraham Lincoln*. Lexington, KY: Henry Clay Memorial Foundation, 1952, 2007.

Keckley, Elizabeth. *Behind the Scenes or Thirty Years a Slave, and Four Years in the White House*. Salem, NH: Azen Co., Publisher, Inc., 1868. Repr., 1985.

Kirwan, Albert D. *John J. Crittenden: The Struggle for the Union*. Lexington: University of Kentucky Press, 1962.

Kleber, John E., editor in chief. *The Kentucky Encyclopedia*. Lexington: University Press of Kentucky, 1992.

Klotter, James C. *The Breckinridges of Kentucky, 1760–1981*. Lexington: University Press of Kentucky, 1986.

Lucas, Marion B. *A History of Blacks in Kentucky: From Slavery to Segregation, 1760–1891*. Kentucky Historical Society, 1992.

Matthews, Gary Robert. *Basil Wilson Duke: The Right Man in the Right Place*. Lexington: University Press of Kentucky, 2005.

McDonough, James Lee. *War in Kentucky: From Shiloh to Perryville*. Knoxville: University of Tennessee Press, 1994.

McQueen, Keven. *Cassius M. Clay: Freedom's Champion*. Paducah, KY: Turner Publishing, 2001.

Milward, Burton, and Burton Milward Jr., trans. and ed. *Reminiscences of 'Aunt Betty' Hummons, written in 1927 (Lexington during the Civil War)*. N.p.: Larkspur Press, 1999. ©Burton Milward Jr.

Neff, Dr. Robert O., and Edith Elizabeth Pollitz. *The Bride and the Bandit*. N.p.: self-published, 1998.

O'Flaherty, Daniel. *General Jo Shelby: The Undefeated Rebel*. Chapel Hill: University of North Carolina Press, 1954.

Peter, Robert, MD. *History of Fayette County Kentucky...* Edited by William Henry Porter. Chicago: O.L. Baskin & Co., Historical Publishers, 1882. (Sections by Ranck.)

———. (Prepared by his daughter Miss Johanna Peter.) *The History of the Medical Department of Transylvania University.* Filson Club Publication #20. Louisville, KY: John P. Morton & Co., 1905.

———. (and his daughter Johanna Peter.) *Transylvania University: Its Origin, Rise, Decline, and Fall.* Filson Club Publication #11. Louisville, KY: John P. Morton & Co., 1896.

Porter, John M. *One of Morgan's Men.* Edited by Kent Masterson Brown. Lexington: University Press of Kentucky, 2011.

Ramage, James A. *Rebel Raider: The Life of General John Hunt Morgan.* Lexington: University Press of Kentucky, 1986.

Remini, Robert V. *At the Edge of the Precipice: Henry Clay and the Compromise that Saved the Union.* New York: Basic Books, 2010.

———. *Henry Clay: Statesman for the Union.* New York: W.W. Norton & Co., 1991.

Richardson, H. Edward. *Cassius Marcellus Clay: Firebrand of Freedom.* Lexington: University Press of Kentucky, 1976.

Rose, Jerlene, ed. *Kentucky's Civil War 1861–1865.* Clay City: Back Home in Kentucky, Inc., 2005.

Ryen, Dag. *Traces: The Story of Lexington's Past.* Lexington, KY: Lexington-Fayette County Historic Commission, 1987.

Schultz, Duane. *The Dahlgren Affair: Terror and Conspiracy in the Civil War.* New York: W.W. Norton & Co., 1998.

Simms, Jere H., ed. *The Last Night and Last Day of John Hunt Morgan's Raid: Eyewitness Accounts of Morgan's Ohio Raid of 1863*. West Jefferson, OH: Genesis Publishing Co., Ltd., 1997.

Smiley, David L. *Lion of White Hall: The Life of Cassius M. Clay*. Madison: University of Wisconsin Press, 1962. Repr. 1969, Peter Smith.

Smith, John David, and William Cooper, Jr., eds. *A Union Woman in Civil War Kentucky: The Diary of Frances Peter*. Lexington: University Press of Kentucky, 2000.

———. *Window on the War: Frances Dallam Peter's Lexington Civil War Diary*. N.p.: Lexington-Fayette County Historic Commission, 1976. Booklet, paper bound.

Steers, Edward, Jr. *Blood on the Moon: The Assassination of Abraham Lincoln*. Lexington: University Press of Kentucky, 2001.

Swanson, James. *Bloody Crimes: The Chase for Jefferson Davis and the Death Pageant for Lincoln's Corpse*. New York: HarperCollins, 2010.

Tallant, Harold D. *Evil Necessity: Slavery and Political Culture in Antebellum Kentucky*. Lexington: University Press of Kentucky, 2003.

Taylor, David L. *"With Bowie Knives & Pistols": Morgan's Raid in Indiana*. Lexington, IN: Taylor Made Write, 1993.

Thomas, Edison H. *John Hunt Morgan and His Raiders*. Lexington: University Press of Kentucky, 1985.

Tidwell, William A. *Come Retribution: The Confederate Secret Service and the Assassination of Lincoln*. Jackson: University Press of Mississippi, 1988.

Townsend, William H. *Lincoln and the Bluegrass: Slavery and the Civil War in Kentucky*. Lexington: University Press of Kentucky, 1955.

Turner, Justin G., and Linda Levitt Turner, eds. *Mary Todd Lincoln: Her Life and Letters*. New York: Fromm International Publishing Corp., 1987.

Vander Heuvel, Gerry. *Crowns of Thorns and Glory: Mary Todd Lincoln and Varina Howell Davis: Two First Ladies of the Civil War*. New York: E.P. Dutton, 1988.

Wagers, Margaret Newman. *The Education of a Gentleman: Jefferson Davis at Transylvania, 1821–1824*. Lexington, KY: Buckley & Reading, 1943.

Warren, Robert Penn. *Jefferson Davis Gets His Citizenship Back*. Lexington: University Press of Kentucky, 1980.

White, Ronald C. *Lincoln's Greatest Speech: The Second Inaugural*. Waterville, ME: Thorndike Press, 2002.

Woodworth, Steven E. *Davis and Lee at War*. Lawrence: University Press of Kansas, 1995.

Wright, John D., Jr. *Lexington, Heart of the Bluegrass*. Lexington, KY: Lexington-Fayette County Historic Commission, 1982.

———. *Transylvania: Tutor to the West*. Lexington, KY: Transylvania University Press, 1975.

Special Materials

Clay, Cassius M. Papers, University of Kentucky Special Collections, Margaret I. King Library.

Cravens, Dennis. Private Collection, including *Civil War Times* magazines, newspapers, maps, memorabilia.

Evans, Catherine Peter. Papers, letters, sketches, memorabilia, University of Kentucky Special Collections, MIK Library.

Gratz, Miriam. Civil War journal in the Evans papers, University of Kentucky Special Collections, MIK Library.

Morgan, John Hunt. Papers, letters, University of Kentucky Special Collections, MIK Library.

"'Our Only Hope Was in Kentucky': The Civil War Sesquicentennial." Civil War exhibit, University of Kentucky Special Collections, MIK Library.

Peter, Frances Dallam. Civil War journals in the Catherine Peter Evans papers, University of Kentucky Special Collections, MIK Library.

Sanders, George N. Political correspondence, University of Kentucky Special Collections, MIK Library.

Squires, Melinda. "The Controversial Career of George Nicholas Sanders," unpublished master's theses and specialist projects, 2000. Paper 704. digitalcommons.wku.edu/theses/704.

Index

About the Authors

Joshua H. Leet has coauthored two books on the compliance and ethics field. He is a lifelong resident of Lexington and a graduate of Transylvania University, where such men as Jefferson Davis, John Hunt Morgan and Cassius Clay studied.

Karen M. Leet has published over six hundred articles and stories in national and regional outlets, including historical articles on a wide range of Kentucky subjects. Examples include articles on Mary Todd and Abraham Lincoln, Kentucky aviation and disasters such as the 1811–12 earthquakes in the New Madrid seismic zone. She has previously worked as University of Kentucky tour director and as a tour guide in the Bluegrass area.

This is the first book for the mother and son duo.

Visit us at
www.historypress.net

www.ingramcontent.com/pod-product-compliance
Lightning Source LLC
Chambersburg PA
CBHW070354100426
42812CB00005B/1500